New Flow Of Spoken English

New Flow Of Spoken English

Jagram Singh

KALPAZ

First Published, 2019

Published by

Kalpaz Publications
C-30, Satyawati Nagar,
Delhi – 110052
E-mail: kalpaz@hotmail.com
Ph.: 9212142040

Printed at: G. Print Process, Delhi

Cataloging in Publication Data—DK
Courtesy: D.K. Agencies (P) Ltd. <docinfo@dkagencies.com>

Singh, Jagram, author.
New flow of spoken English / Jagram Singh.
pages cm
ISBN 9789386397195

1. English language—Spoken English. 2. English language—Conversation and phrase books. 3. English language—Grammar. I. Title.

LCC PE1074.8.S56 2019 | DDC 428.3 23

A NEW FLOW ON CONVERSATION

"LANGUAGE IS THE GLORIOUS HISTORY AND CONSTANT IDENTITY OF THE LAND, PEOPLE AND THE CULTURE OF ANY HEAVENLY NATION."

OR IT IS A SILENT REPLY OF CIVILISATION IN THE UNIVERSE.

Contents

Messages

This book will help the students to use and understand the language. The detailed information about the language in the form of the grammar will provide an ample guidance and practice in sentence building, correct usage of English language structures as well.

I assume so

With best wishes

Yours

Dr. Ganesh Gupta
M.A. Ph.D. English
Jiwaji university Gwalior
Post – U.D.T. Govt. Excellence
H.S.S. Kailaras
Dist. – Morena (M.P.)

I read your book. I think your book is very useful for those who want to enlarge their knowledge in English for conversation and basic grammar. I am very much impressed with your book. If I have a chance to meet you I would meet you and share your experience to shine my life.

I am very much obliged you.

With best wishes

Yours

Jayvir Singh Jadon
M.A. English, B.Ed.
Principal Govt. Exe. School Kailaras
Distt. Morena (M.P.)

I got through this book and found it very helpful for those students who have less knowledge of English. The language of the book is very simple itself and can easily be understand by the readers without guidance of other experts. Having use of different words, sentences and meanings make it different from other grammar books.

With best wishes

Yours

Mukesh Kumar Dhakad
M.A. English, B.Ed.
Jiwaji University Gwalior
Senior Teacher (English)
Govt. H.S.S. Sujarma
Morena (M.P.)

Preface

I have seen many people speak English in a self-conscious way. It is apparent that they are not sure of themselves. No doubt that they have the required stock of words yet they fumble. In their inner mind they think they can strike up and keep on a conversation but they are found to be withdrawn. If this is the case with you too, this book will help you provide the needed assistance.

People who have a little knowledge of English can have a great deal of exposure to English if they take conscious effort to study this book. That is the reader of this book ought to speak each conversation rhythmically at least ten times aloud and his/her fluency is certain to develop. When we emotionally utter sentences like. "Haven't I told you umpteen number of times not indulge in such acts of back-biting", our organs of speech require more blood supply. When sufficient blood is not supplied, our communication becomes a written style.

In other words there is lack fluency of What I mean is simply this. Emotion connotes rhythm and vice-versa. That is, don't just read the conversation, for form's sake, speak it, that too aloud raising and bringing down your voice wherever required. The benefits will be doubled if it is practised in front of a life-size mirror. If this speaking aloud is followed by making at least 4 similar conversations wherever possible, our aim of speaking English becomes further easier since our critical faculties are likely to be sharpened. Result, our faculty will be adapted to the language we are learning: We hope that more advanced learners and teachers will also find it useful.

I have attained every nerve to develop my fluency because I studied in vernacular medium. This book is based on my experience of teaching Spoken English over a long period. At least I fervently hope that this book helps one to speak good English if not an impeccable variety. Suggestions if any to enhance the Quality of this book are always welcome.

We wish to thank all who have assisted in the preparation of the first addition. We would also like to thank all colleagues for their friendly and helpful suggestions.

Jagram Singh

Golden Rules for Spoken English

'The Golden Rules of Spoken English' provides a potential learner with a handful of essential rules to practice speaking English. This write-up identifies some tried and tested rules to improve spoken English skills and explains them with examples. The list includes helpful tips for building vocabulary, individual speaking styles and confidence level. One can learn a language most effectively through a practice-based approach rather than just learning the rules. Learners can follow these points as a checklist and utilize each one of them for effective communication:

1. When to build your vocabulary: First focus on speaking English and listening to English with whatever vocabulary you have; once you are comfortable in speaking and understanding, then start building advanced vocabulary.

2. The importance of grammar: You can speak English even if you have little knowledge of grammar. Do you remember your childhood when you started speaking Hindi or your mother tongue without going to school and without learning any grammar? Moreover, there are thousands of people who never attended school and can speak their mother tongues or other languages comfortably.

3. Do not blame your atmosphere: If you do not want to do something, it is easy to blame your circumstances. But the fact is that you can always create your own situations. For example, if you say that you do not have any friend to speak English, you can practice before the mirror. Another example would be saying, that no one speaks English at your home watch TV and listen to people who speak English.

4. Practice before the mirror: When you practice speaking English with your friend, you cannot watch your confidence level- and facial expression. But when you practice before the mirror. You can always evaluate your confidence level, observe your facial expressions and body.

5. Using a dictionary with pronunciation: When you start speaking English, you always fear to mispronounce words. You can overcome this fear by listening to people who speak good English and buying a dictionary with CD for pronunciation so that you can understand and copy correct pronunciation.

6. Observe different speaking styles: Everyone wants to develop a good style of speaking. The best way to develop this is to observe and listen to people who speak good English.

7. Practice different tones of voice: To develop confidence in speaking it is a best to practice speaking a single sentence in different tones, You will feel comfortable if you practice speaking in different tones, i.e., speak confidently for two minutes speak angrily for two minutes.

8. Record yourself: For better results, audiotape or videotape yourself. Find out what you really like in your speaking style and make it stronger: if you feel that you need to improve something in your speaking, work on that also.

9. Speak without fear: Last but not the least, you cannot make a good impression with a shaky voice, so always make sure you speak with confidence. Just like your favourite artist in a movie who speaks with power and authority in his/her voice, try to articulate your speech.

1st Day

1.	वाह वाह!	Marvellous!
2.	शाबाश!	Well done!
3.	अति सुंदर!	Beautiful!
4.	अरे!	Oh!
5.	हाय!	Woe!/ Alas!
6.	हरे राम!	O God!
7.	आपने तो कमाल कर दिया!	Done Wonderful!
8.	बेशक!	Certainly!
9.	ईश्वर को धन्यवाद!	Thank God!
10.	ईश्वर की कृपा से!	By God's grace!
11.	खुदा आप को बरकत दे!	May god bless you!
12.	आपको भी!	Same to you!
13.	बहुत बढ़िया!	Excellent!
14.	बड़े दुख का समाचार!	A matter of great sorrow!
15.	कितनी बड़ी विजय!	What a great victory!
16.	हे प्रभु!	My goodness!
17.	सुनिये!	Hello!
18.	फटाफट करिये!	Hurry up Please!
19.	कितना भयानक!	How terrible!
20.	कितने अपमान की बात है!	How disgraceful!

21. बड़ी फिजूल की बात है!	How absurd!
22. क्या खूब!	How sweet!
23. उसकी इतनी हिम्मत!	How dare he!
24. कितना सुंदर!	How beautiful!
25. ऐसा कहने की तुम्हारी हिम्मत कैसे हुई!	How dare you say that!
26. प्यारे!	Oh dear!
27. जल्दी चलो!	Hurry up!
28. चुप रहिए!	Quiet Please!
29. हां ऐसा ही!	Exactly so!
30. सचमुच!	Really!
31. सच!	Indeed!
32. धन्यवाद!	Thanks!
33. आपका धन्यवाद!	Thank you!
34. भगवान का लाख शुक्र है!	Thank God!
35. यह दिन बार बार आए!	Many happy returns of the day!
36. अहहा! मैंने जीत लिया!	Hurrah! I won!
37. आपके स्वास्थ्य के लिए!	To your good health!
38. आपकी सफलता पर बधाई!	Congratulations on your success!
39. कितनी बेहूदिगी है!	What a nonsense!
40. कितनी शर्म की बात है!	What a shame!
41. कितनी दुःखद बात है!	What a tragedy!
42. कितना आश्चर्य!	What a surprise!
43. आश्यर्चजनक!	Wonderful!
44. छिः छिः!	Nasty!
45. खबरदार!, सावधान!	Beware!
46. कितने अफसोस की बात है!	What a pity!

47. कितनी बढ़िया सूझ!	What an idea!
48. स्वागत श्रीमान का!	Welcome sir!
49. हे राम! या खुदा!	O God!
50. बधाई हो!	Congratulations!

Note: Do the practice above given Sentences.

2nd Day

(A)

1.	मैं अभी आ रहा हूँ!	Just coming!
2.	बहुत अच्छा!	Very well!
3.	अच्छी बात है!	All right!
4.	जैसी आपकी मर्जी!	As you wish!
5.	और कुछ?	Anything else?
6.	बस रहने दो!	Enough!
7.	इस सम्मान के लिए धन्यवाद!	Thanks for this honour!
8.	अच्छा!	O.K.!
9.	क्यों नहीं!	Why not!
10.	थोड़ा सा भी नहीं!	Not a bit!
11.	अच्छा चलें।	Ta Ta!
12.	कल देखेंगे!	Till tomorrow!
13.	हां, अवश्य!	Yes by all means!
14.	बहुत है!	Too much!
15.	हां, जनाब!	Yes, sir!
16.	नहीं, कभी नहीं!	No, never!
17.	कोई बात नहीं!	Never mind!
18.	और कुछ नहीं!	Nothing more!
19.	कोई खास बात नहीं!	Please don't mention it!

20. स्वागत है!	Welcome!
21. भरोसा रखें!	Rest assured!/ Have patience.
22. नमस्ते सलाम राम राम सत् सत् श्री अकाल!	Good Morning, Noon, Evening!
23. अच्छा विदा!	Good bye!
24. आपको भी विदा!	Bye Bye!

(B)

1. रुको!	Stop!
2. बोलो!	Speak!
3. सुनो!	Listen!
4. यहां ठहरो!	Stand here!
5. इधर आओ!	Come here!
6. इधर देखो!	Look here!
7. यह लो!	Take this!
8. पास आओ!	Come near!
9. बाहर प्रतीक्षा करो!	Wait outside!
10. ऊपर जाओ!	Go up!
11. नीचे जाओ!	Go down!
12. उतर जाओ!	Get down!
13. तैयार हो जाओ!	Be ready!/ Get ready.
14. चुप रहो!	Be silent!
15. सावधान रहो!	Be careful!
16. धीरे चलो!	Go slowly!
17. तुरन्त जाओ!	Go at once! or Go right now!
18. सीधे जाओ!	Go straight!
19. चले जाओ!	Go away!
20. अच्छी तरह साफ करो!	Clean properly!

21. मत जाओ! — Do not go!
22. मत भूलो! — Do not forget!
23. इसे मत तोड़ो! — Do not break it!
24. मुझे मत सताओ! — Do not trouble me!
25. फिर कोशिश करो! — Do try again!

Note:- सभी वाक्यों के पूर्व Please जोड़ें परन्तु अधिकारी के लिए Kindly जोड़ें तभी पूर्ण होंगे।

3rd Day

(A)

1.	सामने देखो!	Look ahead!
2.	आगे बढ़ो!	Go ahead!
3.	गाड़ी धीरे चलाओ!	Drive slowly!
4.	उनका नाम पूछो!	Ask his name!
5.	अपना काम करो!	Mind your business!
6.	वापस जाओ!	Go back!
7.	वापस आओ!	Come back!
8.	सुनिये तो!	Just listen!
9.	जल्दी आना!	Come soon!
10.	मुझे देखने दो!	Let me see!
11.	मुझे काम करने दो!	Let me work!
12.	इसे जाने दीजिए!	Let him pass!
13.	मुझे जाने दो!	Let me go!
14.	तैयार रहना!	Be ready!
15.	उसकी खबर रखना!	Take care of her!
16.	एक तरफ हो जाओ!	Move aside!
17.	सोच समझकर बोलो!	Think before you speak!
18.	अवश्य आना!	Do come!

(B)

19. मजाक मत करो!	Don't cut jokes!
20. बेहूदा न बको!	Do not talk nonsense!
21. कुछ परवाह न करो!	Never mind!
22. देर मत करो!	Do not delay!
23. कभी मत भूलो!	Never forget!
24. फिक्र मत करो!	Do not worry!
25. उसे मत चिढ़ाओ!	Do not tease him!

(C)

26. कोशिश करो!	Please try!
27. बस रहने दीजिए!	Let it be!
28. जरा ठहरिये!	Please wait!
29. यहां आइए!	Please come here!
30. आइए पधारिये!	Please come in!
31. जरा इन्हें जगाइए!	Please wake him up!
32. विराजिऐ!	Please be seated!
33. उत्तर दीजिए!	Please give me reply!
34. मुझे जाने की इजाजत दीजिए!	Please allow me to go!
35. यहां हस्ताक्षर कीजिए!	Please sign here!
36. जरा और ठहरिये!	Please stay a little longer!
37. मौन रहिए!	Be quiet please!
38. फिर आइएगा!	Please come again!

(D)

40. अपना घर साफ रखो!	Keep your home clean!
41. असली बात पर आओ, इधर उधर की बाते छोड़ो!	Come on the point Do not beat about the bush!
42. देर मत करना!	Don't be late!

43. यह खुराक पियो!	Take this dose!
44. मेरे पीछे आओ!	Follow me!
45. जूतों के तस्मे/फीते बांध लो!	Do up your shoes!
46. जगह खाली करो!	Leave the place!
47. कुछ मत कहो!	Don't say anything!
48. उस शैतान को देखो!	See the devil!
49. उचित समय पर प्रयास करो!	Strike when the iron is hot!
50. काम के समय काम करो खेल के समय खेलो!	Work while you work, and play while you play!

4th Day

(A)

	Correct	Incorrect
1.	Your pen please.	Give me your pen.
2.	A glass of water, please.	Give me a glass of water.
3.	Time please?	What is the time?
4.	Yes, Please.	Yes I will drink.
5.	A chance please.	Give me a chance.
6.	Allow please.	Give me allow.
7.	Rate please?	What is the rate?
8.	Cost please?	What is the cost?
9.	Your book please.	Give me your book.
10.	Your aim please?	What is your aim?

(B)

11. Thank you या thanks, या Many many thanks to you या Thank you very much.
12. मैं और नहीं लेना चाहता I do not want more इसके बदले या No. thanks.
13. Thanks या Thank you के बदले में बोलें Its all right या No mention या Welcome या You're welcome.
14. ले लीजिए Take it के बदले में With great pleasure.
15. मुझे अवसर दें Allow me ही बोलें
16. पहले आप First you के बदले में After you बोले।

(C)

17. किसी से हाथ छू जाये या अचानक टकरा जाये तो बोलें — Sorry
18. आपको बीच से या रास्ते से जाना हो तो बोलें — Excuse me
19. यदि बात समझ नहीं आ रहीं हो तो Pardon या Sorry बोलो
20. May I come in sir का उत्तर दें Certainly या Of course या With great pleasure.

(D)

21. साधारण क्षमा करना।	Excuse
22. ह्दय से क्षमा करना।	Forgive
23. दण्डभोग से मुक्त करना।	Pardon
24. गलती स्वीकार करना।	Apologize
25. दुःखित के लिए।	Sorry
26. भूल से।	By mistake
27. कृपया दुबारा कहें।	Please repeat it

5th Day

(A)

वर्णों का उच्चारण

1. A (अ, आ, ए, ऐ)
2. B (ब)
3. C (क, स)
4. D (ड)
5. E (इ, ए)
6. F (फ)
7. G (ग, ज)
8. H (ह)
9. I (ई–ई, आई)
10. J (ज)
11. K (क)
12. L (ल)
13. M (म)
14. N (न)
15. O (ओ)
16. P (प)
17. Q (क)
18. R (र)
19. S (स)
20. T (ट)
21. U (आ, उ, ऊ, यू)
22. V (व)
23. W (व)
24. X (एक्स)
25. Y (य, आइ)
26. Z (ज)

(B)

1. Ch च, Th थ ठ, Ph फ, Sh श, Gh घ, Gh के पूर्व दीर्घ स्वर होता Gh का उच्चारण Silent होता है। जैसे Right राइट
2. Q के साथ सदा U लगता है।

6th Day

(स्वरों के उच्चारण)

1. (A)

ऐ – Lad, man

आ – Call, small

ए य – Fare, Dare

ए – Pay, way

2. (E)

ए – Net, sell

ई – Be, He

ई – See, weep

ई – Clean, meat

Note:- यदि किसी शब्द के अंत में आये तो उसका कोई उच्चारण या ध्वनि नहीं होती।

3. (I)

इयू – New, few

इ – Big, kill

आई – Kind, mild

आई – Right, might

अ – First, firm

आय – Fire, Admire

ई – Receive, sieve

4. (O)

ऑ	–	Ox, oh
ओ	–	Open, hope
ओ	–	Low, row
उ	–	Look, book
ऊ	–	Room, boot
अ	–	Come, son
आउ	–	Cow, now
वाय	–	Joy, toy

5. (U)

अव – आव	–	Hour, sour
ऊ	–	Up, tub
उ	–	Pull, push

6. (Y)

यू–ओ	–	Duty, cure, sure, hurdle
ई–ए–आई	–	Ready, gay, cry, type
आय	–	Try

7th Day

व्यंजनों के उच्चारण
Pronunciation of Consonants

1. (C के उच्चारण)

1. C के बाद E, I, Y आये तो 'स' होगा।
   Icy, Cinema, Celebrate, Century, Circle, etc.
2. C के बाद a, o, u, k, आये तो 'क' होगा।
   Cot, Cat, Cut, Cock, etc.
3. कभी कभी C के बाद IA, EA हो तो 'श' होगा।
   Social, Ocean, Musician, etc.

2. (G के उच्चारण)

1. जब शब्दों के अंत में GE हो तो 'ज' होगा।
   Page, Cage, Sage, Age, Rage, etc.
2. यदि शब्द के अंत में GI हो तो कभी कभी 'ज' बोला जाता है।
   Ginger, Imagine, etc.
3. शेष स्थानों पर 'ग' उच्चारण होता है।
   Big, Bag, Hang, Gold, Hunger, Give, etc.

3. (S के उच्चारण)

1. जब शब्दों के अंत में be, g, gg, ge, oe, ie, ee, y आये तो और इनके बाद S लगे तो उच्चारण 'ज' होगा।
   Tribes, Bags, Eggs, Ages, Heroes, Stories, Rupees, Toys, Rays, etc.

2. यदि शब्द के अंत में F, P, PE, KE, GHT, TE वर्ण S का उच्चारण 'स' होगा।

   Roofs, clipse, Hopes, Kites, Ships, Jokes Nights etc.

9. यदि शब्द में S या SS के बाद IA, ION हो तो प्रायः S का उच्चारण 'श' होगा।

   Aggression, Asia, Pension, Session, Russia, Mansion etc.

4. (T के उच्चारण)

1. यदि T के बाद IA, IO, IE, हो तो T का उच्चारण 'श' होगा।
   Initial, Patient, Portion, Promotion, Ratio etc.

2. यदि S के बाद tion या T के बाद ure आये तो 'च' होगा।
   Question, Culture, Nature, Future etc.

3. यदि T के बाद H आये तो 'थ' या 'द' होगा।
   Thick, Thin, This, That, Three, Then etc.

4. कई बार Th का उच्चारण 'ट' होता है।
   Thames टेम्स, Thomas टॉमस etc.

5. 1. स्वर से शुरु होने वाले शब्द के साथ The 'दि' बोला जाता है।
   The answer, the apples etc.

2. व्यंजन से शुरु होने वाले शब्द के साथ 'द' बोला जाता है।
   The question, the cats etc.

8th Day

1.	(C-Silent)	Scent, science, scene, etc.
2.	(G-Silent)	Sign, design, resign etc.
3.	(H-Silent)	Honour, hour, Thomas etc.
4.	(K-Silent)	Knock, knife, knot etc.
5.	(L-Silent)	Palm, calm, half, calf, etc. Folk, talk, should, would, could etc.
6.	(N-Silent)	Autumn, condemn, hymn, column etc.
7.	(T-Silent)	Hasten, listen often, soften etc.
8.	(U-Silent)	Guard, guess, guest etc.
9.	(W-Silent)	Wrong, answer, sword etc.

9th Day

1. कृपया अंदर आइए।	Come in please.
2. कृपया कुछ ठंडा लिजिए।	Please have a cold drink.
3. टहलने के लिए आइए।	Come for a walk please.
4. आओ बस से चले।	Let us go by bus.
5. कहो दोस्त कैसे हो?	Hello friend how are you?
6. बहुत बढ़िया, शुक्रिया आपका।	Very well, thank you.
7. मैं ठीक ठाक हूँ।	I am fine.
8. आपसे मिलकर मुझे बड़ी प्रसन्नता हुई।	I am glad to see you.
9. यह मेरे लिए खुशी की बात है।	The pleasure is all mine.
10. बहुत दिनों बाद मिले है।	It is a long time since we meet
11. मैंने आपके बारे में बहुत सुना हैं।	I have heard a lot about you.
12. देखो कौन है?	Look, who is it?
13. क्या आप मुझे देखकर चकित हो रहे हो?	Are you surprised to see me?
14. अच्छा फिर मिलेंगे।	Okay, till we meet again.
15. क्या आप अब अवश्य जायेंगे।	Must you go now.
16. आपकी यात्रा अच्छी हों।	Have a good journey.
17. ईश्वर आप पर कृपा करें।	God bless you.
18. भाग्य आपका साथ दें।	May luck favour you.

19. अच्छा चलें श्रीमान (रात को)।	Good night friend.
20. नमस्ते श्रीमान।	Bye Bye.
21. अनेक धन्यवाद।	Many thanks.
22. आपकी सलाह के लिए धन्यवाद।	Thanks for your advice.
23. आपके निमंत्रण के लिए धन्यवाद।	Thanks for your invitation.
24. मैं आपका बहुत अनुग्रहीत हूँ।	I am very grateful to you.
25. भेंट के लिए धन्यवाद।	Thanks for the present.
26. मैं आपका बहुत आभारी हूँ।	I am much obliged to you.
27. आप बहुत कृपालू हैं।	You are very kind.
28. हम आपके लिए नये वर्ष की शुभकामना करते हैं।	We wish you a happy new year.
29. आपके जन्मदिन पर हार्दिक अभिनंदन।	Hearty felicitation on your birthday.
30. यह दिन बार बार आये।	Many happy returns of the day.
31. आपकी सफलता पर बधाई।	Congratulation on your success.
32. आपका लोक और परलोक सुखी हो।	May you have the best of both the world.
33. आप पर भाग्य सदा कृपालू हों।	May good fortune always smile upon you.
34. फलो – फूलो।	May you flourish.
35. मैं आपको सब की ओर से बधाई देता हूँ।	I congratulate you on behalf of all.

10th Day

(A)

1. नौ बजे है।	It is a nine o' clock.
2. सवा नौ बजे है।	It is a quarter past nine o' clock.
3. पौने नौ बजे है।	It is a quarter to nine o' clock.
4. साढ़े नौ बजे है।	It is a half past nine o' clock.
5. नौ बजकर दस मिनट है।	It is a ten minutes past nine o' clock.
6. नौ बजने में दस मिनट शेष है।	It is a ten minutes to nine o' clock.

(B)

7. शुरु करें?	Shall we begin?
8. मैं भी चलूं?	May I go?
9. मैं भी चलूं?	May I join you?
10. अच्छा आज्ञा दीजिए।	Well, allow me to go.
11. मुझे जाने दो।	Let me go.
12. अब आप जा सकते है।	You may go now.
13. क्या मैं टेलिफोन कर लूं?	May I use your phone?
14. क्या मैं बिजली बंद कर दूं?	May I switch off the light?
15. क्या मैं अन्दर आ सकता हूँ?	May I come in, please?
16. हां बड़ी खुशी से।	Yes, with great pleasure.
17. क्या मैं यहां थोड़ा सुस्ता लूं?	May I rest here for a while?

(C)

18. आप अपना काम करें।	Go about your business.
19. यह कोट पहन कर देखों।	Try this coat on.
20. दिल लगाकर काम करो।	Work wholeheartedly.
21. तनिक नर्मी से बात करों।	Talk politely.
22. इस पत्र को देखते ही उत्तर दो।	Reply by return of post.
23. हिसाब की देखभाल कर लो।	Check the accounts.
24. अपने आपको सुधार लो।	Mend your ways.
25. मेरे साथ पैर मिलाकर चलो।	Keep pace with me.
26. बच्चे को सुला दो।	Put the child to bed.
27. संभल कर चलना।	Walk cautiously.

(D)

28. तुम्हीं जाओ।	Go yourself.
29. तैयार रहना।	Be ready.
30. दीया जलाना।	Light the lamp.
31. बिजली जला दो।	Switch on the light.
32. दीया बुझा दो।	Put off the lamp.
33. हाथ धोना।	Wash your hands.
34. देर मत करो।	Don't delay.
35. दूसरों की नकल न करो।	Do not ape others.
36. जाओ नाक साफ करो।	Go and blow your nose.
37. विस्तार से पत्र लिखो।	Write a detailed letter.
38. भविष्य में ऐसा मत करना।	Do not do so in future.
39. समय का पालन करो।	Be punctual.
40. बक बक न करो।	Don't chatter.
41. मूर्ख मत बनो।	Don't be silly.
42. अतिथियों की सेवा करो।	Entertain the guests.

43. देश सेवा में जाने दो। — Lay down your life in the service of motherland.

44. काम में रुकावट मत डालो। — Do not hold up the work.

(E)

45. विश्वास रखिये। — Rest assured.

46. अपनी चिंता मिटाओ। — Stop worrying.

47. डरने की कोई बात नहीं। — There is nothing to fear.

48. मेरी चिंता न करो। — Don't worry about me.

49. डरो मत। — Don't be afraid.

50. हिचकिचाओ मत। — Don't hesitate.

51. मुझे इसकी परवाह नहीं। — I don't care for this.

52. मुझे आप पर गर्व है। — I am proud of you.

53. कोई हर्ज नहीं। — It doesn't matter.

54. घबराओ मत। — Don't get nervous.

55. बड़े अफसोस की बात हैं। — It's a pity.

56. उसे सांत्वना दो। — Console him.

(F)

57. मेरे भाई भाग्य से कौन लड़ सकता है। — My brother who can stand against life/fate.

58. ईश्वर की यही इच्छा थी। — It was inexorable.

59. हमारी आपसे सहानुभूति है। — We sympathies with you.

60. हम अपनी संवेदना प्रकट करते हैं। — We offer our condolences.

61. किसका दोष है? — Who is to blame?

62. कैसी शर्म की बात है! — What a shame!

63. मैं किसका विश्वास करुं? — Whom should I trust?

64. यह मेरा कसूर नहीं है। — It was not my fault.

65. उसने नाक में दम कर रखा है।	He is a thorough nuisance.
66. उसने मेरे विश्वास को ठेस पहुंचाई हैं।	He has let me down.
67. मुझे उससे चिढ़ आती है।	He irritates me.
68. वह अपनी बात का धनी नहीं है।	He is not a man of his word.
69. उसने मुझे धोखा दिया।	He has cheated me.
70. मुझे क्रोध मत चढ़ाओ।	Do not make me lose my temper.
71. वह गधा है।	He is a duffer.
72. कमाल कर दिया।	That's wonderful.
73. तुम कितने अच्छे हो।	You are so nice / You are awfully nice.

11th Day

1.	ऐसा नहीं है।	It is not so.
2.	मुझे कुछ नहीं चाहिए।	I want nothing.
3.	यह नहीं हो सकता।	It cannot be.
4.	मैं नहीं मानता।	I do not agree.
5.	जिद्दी मत बनो।	Do not be obstinate.
6.	मैं इसे सहन नहीं कर सकती।	Sorry, I can't afford.
7.	गुस्सा न कीजिए।	Don't be angry.
8.	कायरता मत दिखाओ।	Do not play a coward.
9.	जैसी आपकी मर्जी।	As you like.
10.	ऐसा ही होगा।	It will be so.
11.	मैं सहमत हूँ।	I agree.
12.	मैं आपसे बिलकुल सहमत हूँ।	I entirely with you.
13.	अपने पिता का कहा करो।	Do your father bidding.
14.	क्षमा करे/माफ करो/माफी चाहती हूँ।	Excuse me.
15.	मुझे यह सुनकर बड़ा दुख हुआ।	I am very sorry to hear this.
16.	मेरी संवेदना स्वीकार करें।	You have all my Sympathy.

12th Day

1. जो हो सो हो।	Come what may.
2. मैंने तुम्हारा क्या बिगाड़ा है।	What harm have I done to you.
3. आवेश मे न आओ।	Don't be excited.
4. क्या आपके होश ठिकाने है?	Are you in your senses?
5. मेरी आंखों से दूर हो जाओ।	Get out of my sight.
6. बात को अधिक न बढ़ाओ।	Don't stretch matters.
7. भाड़ में जाओ।	Go to hell.
8. झगड़े का फैसला हो गया।	The matter ends.
9. आप नाराज हो गये।	Are you angry.
10. मैं तो मजाक कर रहा था।	I was just joking.
11. मुझे यह जानकर दुख हुआ।	I was pained to hear this.
12. मैं आपसे माफी चाहता हूँ।	I beg your pardon.
13. मुझे बहुत अफसोस है।	I am very sorry.
14. यह अनजाने में हुआ था।	It was done inadvertently.
15. यह आपका दोष नहीं है।	It was not your fault.
16. कोई हर्ज नहीं।	That's all right.
17. चुल्लूभर पानी में डूब मरो। या दफा हो जाओ।	Get lost.
18. तुम्हें शर्म आनी चाहिए।	You should be ashamed of yourself
19. तुम बड़े चालू आदमी हो।	You are very slippery character.

20. लानत है तुम पर।	Shame on you.
21. तुम बड़े नीच/धूर्त हो।	You are just too cunning.
22. यह सब तुम्हारी करतूत है।	This is all your doing.
23. तुम उससे बच नहीं सकते।	You cannot get away from this.
24. उसके जिम्मेदार तुम हो।	You blame for this. OR You're responible for this.

13th Day

1. दूध फट गया है।	Milk has turned sour.
2. कमरे में सफाई चाहिए।	The room requires cleaning.
3. आपके कितने बाल बच्चे है?	How many children do you have?
4. गीले कपड़े धूप में डाल दो।	Put wet clothes in the sun.
5. मै जरा तैयार हो लूं।	Let me get ready.
6. तुम बड़ी देर लगा रहे हो।	You are taking too long.
7. मुझे नींद आ रही है।	I am feeling sleepy.
8. अंदर कोई नहीं है।	There is no one inside.
9. बस अब सो जाओ।	Go and sleep now.
10. मैं अभी तैयार होता हूँ।	I shall be ready in a moment.
11. मैं जरा आराम कर लूं।	I will rest for a while.
12. आप अभी तक जाग रहे हो।	You are still awake!
13. आपसे कोई मिलने आया है।	Some one has come to see you.
14. आज कल मेरा हाथ तंग है।	I am hard up these days.
15. मैं बहुत थका हूँ।	I am dead tired.
16. आओ गप्प लगाये।	Let us have chat.
17. आप तो ऊंघ रहे है।	You are dozing.
18. तुम्हारी नाक बह रही है।	Your nose is running.
19. मेरा बिछौना कर दो।	Make my bed.
20. द्वार की चटकनी लगा दो।	Bolt the door.

14th Day

(A)

1. उन्होंने आपको याद किया है।	He remembers you.
2. आपका बड़ा इंतजार किया।	I waited long for you.
3. कोई अच्छी खबर सुनाइए।	Let's have some good news.
4. जाते ही पत्र लिखना।	Write immediately on your reaching.
5. कहीं भूल न जाना।	Don't forget about it.
6. उधार कभी मत खरीदो।	Don't buy on credit.
7. मेरा हिसाब चुका दो।	Clear my accounts.
8. क्या माल अच्छा है?	Is the stuff all right?
9. रंग पक्का है?	Is the colour fast?
10. बहुत दूर।	It is quite far.
11. इसमें जंग लगा हुआ है।	It is rusted.
12. यह मैला है।	It is soiled.
13. यह फटा हुआ है।	It is torn.
14. यह बिलकुल नया है।	It is brand new.

(B)

15. आज तो बड़ी गर्मी है।	It is smeltering hot today or it is sunny today.
16. दिन प्रतिदिन सर्दी बढ़ रही है।	It is getting colder day by day.

17. मैं ठिठुर रहा हूँ।	I am shivering.
18. भंयकर दर्द है।	The dust is terrible.
19. हवा में खुनकी है।	There is a nip in the air.
20. मूसलाधार वर्षा हो रही है।	It is raining cats and dogs.
21. उमस बहुत बढ़ गई है।	It is very humid.
22. हवा लगभग बंद है।	The wind is almost still.
23. मीठी हवा चल रही है।	The wind is sitting fair.

15th Day

(A)

1.	आपका शुभ नाम।	Your good name, please.
2.	आपका परिचय।	Who are you please?
3.	न उधार दो न लो।	Neither borrow nor lend.
4.	न धोखा दो न खाओ।	Neither deceive nor be deceived.
5.	सिर्फ नेक आदमी ही सुखी है।	The virtuous alone are happy.
6.	जिन्दगी सेवा के लिए है।	Life is for service.
7.	किसी से कुछ न मांगो।	Don't ask anybody for anything.
8.	आराम हराम है।	To rest is to nust.
9.	निस्वार्थ सेवा में बड़ा आनंन्द है।	There is great joy in selfless service.
10.	उसने अपने पाप का प्रायश्चित कर डाला।	He has atoned for his sin.

(B)

11.	इतना काफी है।	This is enough / that will do.
12.	आपकी कृपा है।	So kind of you.
13.	आपकी बड़ी कृपा होगी।	It would be very kind of you.
14.	मैं आपकी क्या सेवा करुं?	What can I do for you?
15.	आपने कैसे कष्ट किया। या यहाँ किस लिए आये?	What brings you here?

16. बस इतना बहुत है। This is quite enough.
17. बुरा ना मानियेगा। Don't take it ill / Don't mind.
18. हम आपके आभारी है। We are obliged to you.
19. आपकी सहायता के लिए धन्यवाद। Thank you for your help.
20. क्षमा कीजिए। Please excuse me.

16th Day

(A)

1. यात्रा लम्बी है।	The journey is long.
2. हम रास्ता भूल गये।	We strayed.
3. हम साथ साथ चलेंगे।	We shall go together.
4. यह आम रास्ता नहीं है।	It is no throughfare.
5. सड़क मरम्मत के लिए बंद है।	The road is closed for repaires.
6. अब आगे अपना स्टेशन है।	The next station is own.
7. काम से जी मत चुराओ।	Do not shirk work.
8. दूसरों की हंसी मत उड़ाओ।	Do not laugh at others.
9. दूसरों पर निर्भर मत रहो।	Do not depend upon others.
10. नंगे पैरों से बाहर मत जाओ।	Do not go out bare foot.
11. अपना संतुलन मत खोओ।	Do not lose your temper.
12. दूसरों के काम मे खलल मत डालो।	Do not disturb others.
13. काम करते हुए मत ऊंघो।	Do not doze while you work.

(B)

14. काम को काम सिखाता है।	Practice makes a man perfect.
15. नारों से आसमान गूंज उठा।	The shouts rent the sky.
16. इनमें तू तू मैं मैं हो पड़ी।	They exchanged hot words.
17. वह हसमुख साथी है।	She is jolly fellow.

18. वह आंसू पीकर रह गया।	He pocketed the insult.
19. वह आज कल बड़ी मौज में है।	He is making merry these days.
20. यह पृथ्वी पर एक स्वर्ग है।	It is a paradise on earth.
21. जंगल में मोती की कदर नहीं होती।	A thing is not valued where it belong.
22. थोथा चना बाजे घना।	An empty vessel makes much noise.
23. खरबूजे को देखकर खरबूजा रंग बदलता है।	Society moulds man.
24. एक और एक ग्यारह होते है।	Union is strength.
25. गधे को गधा खुजलाता है।	Fools praise fools.
26. एकता बड़ी चीज है।	Union is strength
27. चार दिन की चांदनी फिर अंधेरी रात।	A nine days wonder.
28. आदमी पेट का कुत्ता।	A man is a slave to his stomach.
29. अपनी गली के कुत्ते भी शेर होते है।	A dog is a lion in his lane.
30. मुँह में राम बगल में छूरी।	A honey tongue, a heart of gall.
31. कांटे से कांटा निकलता है।	One nails drives another.
32. मोती गहरे पानी में होता है।	Truth lies at the bottom of a well.
33. जवानी दीवानी होती है।	Youth must have its fling.
34. हर चीज का वक्त होता है।	There is a time for all things.
35. झूठ का अंत नहीं।	One lie leads to another.
36. ताली दोनों हाथों से बजती है।	It takes two to make a quarrel.
37. मित्र वही जो दुखी वक्त में काम आये।	A friend in need is friend indeed.

17th Day

1 – Present Indefinite Tense

1. **Positive Sentences:-**

1. वह जाता है।	He goes.
2. वह खाती है।	She eats.
3. राम पढ़ता है।	Ram reads.
4. सीता खेलती है।	Sita plays.
5. लड़का दौड़ता है।	The boy runs.
6. लड़की गाती है।	The girl sings.
7. मैं आता हूँ।	I come.
8. हम नहाते है।	We take bath.
9. तुम सुनते हो।	You hear.
10. वे बजाते है।	They play.
11. लड़के हंसते है।	The boys laugh.
12. लड़कियाँ देखती है।	The girls look.

2. **Negative Sentences:-**

1. वह नहीं जाता है।	He does not go.
2. वह नहीं खाती है।	She does not eat.
3. राम नहीं पढ़ता है।	Ram does not read.
4. सीता नहीं खेलती है।	Sita does not play.
5. लड़का नहीं दौड़ता है।	The boy does not run.

6.	लड़की नहीं गाती है।	The girl does not sing.
7.	मैं नहीं आता हूँ।	I do not come.
8.	हम नहीं नहाते है।	We do not take bath.
9.	तुम नहीं सुनते हो।	You do not hear.
10.	वे नहीं बजाते है।	They do not playon.
11.	लड़के नहीं हंसते है।	The boys do not laugh.
12.	लड़कियाँ नहीं देखती है।	The girls do not look.

18th Day

3. Interrogative Positive Sentences:-

1.	क्या वह जाता है?	Does he go?
2.	क्या वह खाती है?	Does she eat?
3.	क्या राम पढ़ता है?	Does Ram read?
4.	क्या सीता खेलती है?	Does Sita play?
5.	क्या लड़का दौड़ता है?	Does the boy run?
6.	क्या लड़की गाती है?	Does the girl sing?
7.	क्या मैं आता हूँ?	Do I come?
8.	क्या हम नहाते है?	Do we take bath?
9.	क्या तुम सुनते हो?	Do you hear?
10.	क्या वे बजाते है?	Do they play on?
11.	क्या लड़के हंसते है?	Do the boys laugh?
12.	क्या लड़कियाँ देखती है?	Do the girls look?

4. Interrogative Negative Sentences:-

1.	क्या वह नहीं जाता है?	Does he not go?
2.	क्या वह नहीं खाती है?	Does she not eat?
3.	क्या राम नहीं पढ़ता है?	Does Ram not read?
4.	क्या सीता नहीं खेलती है?	Does Sita not play?
5.	क्या लड़का नहीं दौड़ता है?	Does the boy not run?
6.	क्या लड़की नहीं गाती है?	Does the girl not sing?

7. क्या मैं नहीं आता हूँ?	Do I not come?
8. क्या हम नहीं नहाते है?	Do we not take bath?
9. क्या तुम नहीं सुनते हो?	Do you not hear?
10. क्या वे नहीं बजाते है?	Do they not play on?
11. क्या लड़के नहीं हंसते है?	Do the boys not laugh?
12. क्या लड़कियाँ नहीं देखती है?	Do the girls not look?

19th Day

5. **Interrogative Positive Sentences:- {with Question words}**

आलोक– What – क्या, When – कब, Where – कहाँ, How – कैसे, Why – क्यों, Who – कौन, Which – किसे, Whom – किसको।

1. वह कहाँ जाता है?	Where does he goes?
2. वह क्या खाती है?	What does she eats?
3. राम क्या पढ़ता है?	What does Ram read?
4. सीता क्या खेलती है?	What does Sita play?
5. लड़का क्यों दौड़ता है?	Why does the boy run?
6. लड़की क्या गाती है?	What does the girl sing?
7. मैं कहां आता हूँ?	Where do I come?
8. हम कब नहाते है?	When do we take bath?
9. तुम एक गीत क्यों सुनते हो?	Why do you hear a song?
10. वे क्या बजाते है?	What do they play on?
11. लड़के क्यों हंसते है?	Why do the boys laugh?
12. लड़कियाँ वहां क्या देखती है?	What do the girls look there?

6. **Interrogative Negative Sentences:- {with Question words}**

1. वह घर क्यों नहीं जाता है?	Why does he not go to home?
2. वह क्या नहीं खाती है?	What does she not eat?
3. राम क्या रोज नहीं पढ़ता है?	What does Ram not read daily?

4.	सीता हॉकी क्यों नहीं खेलती है?	Why does Sita not play hockey?
5.	लड़का कहाँ नहीं दौड़ता है?	Where does the boy not run?
6.	लड़की गीत कब नहीं गाती है?	When does the girl not sing a song?
7.	मैं वहां क्यों नहीं आता हूँ?	What do I not come there?
8.	हम कैसे नहीं नहाते है?	How do we not take bath?
9.	तुम क्या नहीं सुनते हो?	What do you not hear?
10.	वे क्या नहीं बजाते है?	What do they not play on?
11.	लड़के तब क्यों नहीं हंसते है?	Why do the boys not laugh then?
12.	लड़कियाँ क्या नहीं देखती है?	What do the girls not look?

20th Day

2 – Past Indefinite Tense

1. **Positive Sentences:-**

1. वह जाता था।	He went.
2. वह खाती थी।	She ate.
3. राम पढ़ता था।	Ram read.
4. सीता खेलती थी।	Sita played.
5. लड़का दौड़ता था।	The boy ran.
6. लड़की गाती थी।	The girl sang.
7. मैं आया।	I came.
8. हम नहाये।	We took bath.
9. तुमने सुना।	You heard.
10. वे बजाते थे ।	They played on.
11. लड़के हंसते थे।	The boys laughed.
12. लड़कियाँ देखती थी।	The girls looked.

2. **Negative Sentences:-**

1. वह नहीं जाता था।	He did not go.
2. वह नहीं खाती थी।	She did not eat.
3. राम नहीं पढ़ता था।	Ram did not read.
4. सीता नहीं खेली।	Sita did not play.
5. लड़का नहीं दौड़ा।	The boy did not run.

6.	लड़की नहीं गाती थी।	The girl did not sing.
7.	मैं नहीं आया।	I did not come.
8.	हम नहीं नहाये।	We did not take bath.
9.	तुमने नहीं सुना।	You did not hear.
10.	वे नहीं बजाते थे।	They did not play on.
11.	लड़के नहीं हंसे।	The boys did not laugh.
12.	लड़कियाँ नहीं देखती थी।	The girls did not look.

21th Day

3. Interrogative Positive Sentences:-

13. क्या वह जाता था?	Did he go?
14. क्या वह खाती था?	Did she eat?
15. क्या राम पढ़ता था?	Did Ram read?
16. क्या सीता खेलती थी?	Did Sita play?
17. क्या लड़का दौड़ता था?	Did the boy run?
18. क्या लड़की गाती थी?	Did the girl sing?
19. क्या मैं आया?	Did I come?
20. क्या हमने नहाया?	Did we take bath?
21. क्या तुमने सुना?	Did you hear?
22. क्या वे बजाते थे?	Did they play?
23. क्या लड़के हंसते थे?	Did the boys laugh?
24. क्या लड़कियाँ देखती थी?	Did the girls look?

4. Interrogative Negative Sentences:-

1. क्या वह नहीं जाता था?	Did he not go?
2. क्या वह नहीं खाती थी?	Did she not eat?
3. क्या राम नहीं पढ़ता था?	Did Ram not read?
4. क्या सीता नहीं खेलती थी?	Did Sita not play?
5. क्या लड़का नहीं दौड़ता था?	Did the boy not run?
6. क्या लड़की नहीं गाती थी?	Did the girl not sing?

7.	क्या मैं नहीं आया?	Did I not come?
8.	क्या हम नहीं नहाये?	Did we not take bath?
9.	क्या तुमने नहीं सुना?	Did you not hear?
10.	क्या वे नहीं बजाते थे?	Did they not playon?
11.	क्या लड़के नहीं हंसते थे?	Did the boys not laugh?
12.	क्या लड़कियाँ नहीं देखती थी?	Did the girls not look?

22nd Day

5. **Interrogative Positive Sentences:- {with Question words}**

आलोक– What – क्या, When – कब, Where – कहाँ, How – कैसे, Why – क्यों, Who – कौन, Which – किसे, Whom – किसको।

1. वह अपना पाठ याद कब करता था? When did he learn his lesson?
2. वह क्या खाती थी? What did she eat?
3. तब कौन पढ़ता था? Who read then?
4. सीता क्या खेलती थी? What did Sita play?
5. लड़का मेंदान में क्यों दौड़ता था? Why did the boy run in the ground?
6. लड़की गीत कैसे गाती थी? How did the girl sing a song?
7. मैं यहां क्यों आया? Why did I come here?
8. हमने आज कितने बजे नहाये? In which time did we take bath?
9. तुमने वहां क्या सुना? What did you hear there?
10. वे क्या बजाते थे? What did they playon?
11. लड़के विद्यालय कब जाते थे? When did the boys go to school?
12. लड़कियाँ क्या देखती थी? What did the girls look?

6. **Interrogative Negative Sentences:- {with Question words}**

1. वह क्या नहीं करता था? What did he not do?
2. वह खाना क्यों नहीं खाती थी? Why did she not eat the

	food?
3. राम ने किसे नहीं मारा था?	Whom did Ram not kill?
4. सीता क्या नहीं खेलती थी?	What did Sita not play?
5. लड़का कहां नहीं दौड़ता था?	Where did the boy not run?
6. लड़की क्या नहीं गाती थी?	What did the girl not sing?
7. मैं घर कब नहीं आया?	When did I not come at home?
8. हम तब क्यों नहीं नहाये?	Why did we not take bath then?
9. तुमने गीत क्यों नहीं सुना?	Why did you not hear a song?
10. वे क्या नहीं बजाते थे?	What did they not playon?
11. लड़के क्यों नहीं हंसते थे?	Why did the boys not laugh?
12. लड़कियाँ क्या नहीं देखती थी?	What did the girls not look?

23rd Day

3 – Future Indefinite Tense

1. Positive Sentences:-

Rule:- Subject + Will/Shall + Verb 1st + object + other words.

आलोक–Shall – केवल I और We के साथ।

Will –शेष सभी कर्ताओं के साथ।

1.	वह जायेगा।	He will go.
2.	वह खायेगी।	She will eat.
3.	राम पढ़ेगा।	Ram will read.
4.	सीता खेलेगी।	Sita will play.
5.	लड़का दौड़ेगा।	The boy will run.
6.	लड़की गायेगी।	The girl will sing.
7.	मैं आऊंगा।	I shall come.
8.	हम नहायेगे।	We shall take bath.
9.	तुम सुनोगे।	You will hear.
10.	वे बजायेंगे।	They will playon.
11.	लड़के हंसेंगे।	The boys will laugh.
12.	लड़कियाँ देखेंगी।	The girls will look.

2. Negative Sentences:-

1.	वह नहीं जायेगा।	He will not go.
2.	वह नहीं खायेगी।	She will not eat.

3.	राम नहीं पढ़ेगा।	Ram will not read.
4.	सीता नहीं खेलेगी।	Sita will not play.
5.	लड़का नहीं दौड़ेगा।	The boy will not run.
6.	लड़की नहीं गायेगी।	The girl will not sing.
7.	मैं नहीं आऊंगा।	I shall not come.
8.	हम नहीं नहायेंगे ।	We shall not take bath.
9.	तुम नहीं सुनोगे।	You will not hear.
10.	वे नहीं बजायेगा।	They will not playon.
11.	लड़के नहीं हंसेगें।	The boys will not laugh.
12.	लड़कियाँ नहीं देखेंगी।	The girls will not look.

24th Day

3. Interrogative Positive Sentences:-

1. क्या वह विद्यालय जायेगा? Will he go to school?
2. क्या वह खाना खायेगी? Will she eat the food?
3. क्या राम पत्र पढ़ेगा? Will Ram read a letter?
4. क्या सीता खेलेगी? Will Sita play?
5. क्या लड़का दौडेगा? Will the boy run?
6. क्या लड़की गायेगी? Will the girl sing?
7. क्या मैं यहां आऊंगा? Shall I come here?
8. क्या हम नहायेंगे? Shall we take bath?
9. क्या तुम सुनोगे? Will you hear?
10. क्या वे बजायेंगे? Will they play?
11. क्या लड़के हंसेंगे? Will the boys laugh?
12. क्या लड़कियाँ देखेंगी? Will the girls look?

4. Interrogative Negative Sentences:-

1. क्या वह नहीं जायेगा? Will he not go?
2. क्या वह नहीं खायेगी? Will she not eat?
3. क्या राम नहीं पढ़ेगा? Will Ram not read?
4. क्या सीता नहीं खेलेगी? Will Sita not play?
5. क्या लड़का नहीं दौड़ेगा? Will the boy not run?
6. क्या लड़की नहीं गायेगी? Will the girl not sing?

7.	क्या मैं नहीं आऊंगा?	Shall I not come?
8.	क्या हम नहीं नहायेंगे?	Shall we not take bath?
9.	क्या तुम नहीं सुनोगे?	Will you not hear?
10.	क्या वे घण्टी नहीं बजायेंगे?	Will they not ring the bell?
11.	क्या लड़के नहीं हंसेंगे?	Will the boys not laugh?
12.	क्या लड़कियाँ नहीं देखेंगी?	Will the girls not look?

25th Day

5. Interrogative Positive Sentences:- {with Question words}

आलोक– What – क्या, When – कब, Where – कहाँ, How – कैसे, Why – क्यों, Who – कौन, Which – किसे, Whom – किसको।

1. वह घर कब जायेगा?	When will he go to home?
2. वह क्या खायेगी?	What will she eat?
3. राम कहां पढ़ेगा?	Where will Ram read?
4. सीता कैसे खेलेगी?	How will Sita play?
5. लड़का क्यों दौड़ेगा?	Why will the boy run?
6. लड़की पत्र कब लिखेगी?	When will the girl write a letter?
7. मैं तुम्हारे बिना कैसे आऊंगा?	How shall I come without you?
8. हम घर पर क्या करेंगे?	What shall we do at home?
9. तुम कार में क्या सुनोगे?	What will you hear in the car?
10. वे क्या बजायेंगे?	What will they play?
11. लड़के अपना काम कब करेंगे?	When will the boys do their work?
12. लड़कियाँ बगीचे में क्या देखेंगी?	What will the girls look in the garden?

6. Interrogative Negative Sentences:- {with Question words}

1. वह मंदिर क्यों नहीं जायेगा?	Why will he not go to temple?
2. वह क्या नहीं खायेगी?	What will she not eat?

3.	राम किताब में क्या नहीं पढ़ेगा?	What will Ram not read in the book?
4.	सीता कबड्डी क्यों नहीं खेलेगी?	Why will Sita not play kabaddi?
5.	राम जंगल में क्यों नहीं दौड़ेगा?	Why will the boy not run in the forest?
6.	लड़की क्या नहीं गायेगी?	What will the girl not sing?
7.	मैं वहां क्यों नहीं आऊंगा?	Why shall I not come there?
8.	हम तालाब में क्यों नहीं नहायेंगे?	Why shall we not take bath in the pond?
9.	तुम कल क्या नहीं सुनोगे?	What will you not hear tomorrow?
10.	वे क्या नहीं बजायेंगे?	What will they not playon?
11.	आज वर्षा क्यों नहीं होगी?	What will it not rain today?
12.	लड़कियाँ क्या नहीं देखेंगी?	What will the girls not look?

26th Day

4 – Present Continuous / Imperfect / Progressive Tense

आलोक– What – क्या, When – कब, Where – कहाँ, How – कैसे, Why – क्यों, Who – कौन, Which – किसे, Whom – किसको।

1. Positive Sentences:-

1. वह जा रहा है।	He is going.
2. वह खा रही है।	She is eating.
3. राम पढ़ रहा है।	Ram is reading.
4. सीता खेल रही है।	Sita is playing.
5. लड़का दौड़ रहा है।	The boy is running.
6. लड़की गा रही है।	The girl is singing.
7. मैं आ रहा हूँ।	I am coming.
8. हम नहा रहे है।	We are bathing.
9. तुम सुन रहे है।	You are hearing.
10. वे बजा रहे है।	They are playing on.
11. लड़के हंस रहे है।	The boys are laughing.
12. वर्षा हो रही है।	It is raining.

2. Negative Sentences:-

1. वह पढ़ने नहीं जा रहा है।	He is not going to study.
2. वह आम नहीं खा रही है।	She is not eating mangoes.
3. राम नहीं पढ़ रहा है।	Ram is not reading.

4. सीता नहीं खेल रही है।	Sita is not playing.
5. लड़का नहीं दौड़ रहा है।	The boy is not running.
6. लड़की नहीं गा रही है।	The girl is not singing.
7. मैं नहीं आ रहा हूँ।	I am not coming.
8. हम नहीं नहा रहे है।	We are not bathing.
9. तुम नहीं सुन रहे है।	You are not hearing.
10. वे नहीं बजा रहे है।	They are not playing on.
11. लड़के नहीं हंस रहे है।	The boys are not laughing.
12. लड़कियाँ फूल नहीं तोड़ रहीं है।	The girls are not plucking the flowers.

27th Day

3. Interrogative Positive Sentences:-

1.	क्या वह जा रहा है?	Is he going?
2.	क्या वह खा रही है?	Is she eating?
3.	क्या राम पढ़ रहा है?	Is Ram reading?
4.	क्या सीता खेल रही है?	Is Sita playing?
5.	क्या लड़का दौड रहा है?	Is the boy running?
6.	क्या लड़की गा रही है?	Is the girl singing?
7.	क्या मैं आ रहा हूँ?	Am I coming?
8.	क्या हम नहा रहे है?	Are we bathing?
9.	क्या तुम सुन रहे हो?	Are you hearing?
10.	क्या वे बजा रहे है?	Are they playing on?
11.	क्या लड़के हंस रहे हैं?	Are the boys laughing?
12.	क्या लड़कियाँ देख रही हैं?	Are the girls looking?

4. Interrogative Negative Sentences:-

1.	क्या वह नहीं जा रहा है?	Is she not going?
2.	क्या वह नहीं खा रही है?	Is she not eating?
3.	क्या राम नहीं पढ़ रहा है?	Is Ram not reading?
4.	क्या सीता नहीं खेल रही है?	Is Sita not playing?
5.	क्या लड़का नहीं दौड़ रहा है?	Is the boy not running?
6.	क्या लड़की नहीं गा रही है?	Is the girl not singing?

7.	क्या मैं नहीं आ रहा हूँ?	Am I not coming?
8.	क्या हम नहीं नहा रहे है?	Are we not taking bath?
9.	क्या तुम नहीं सुन रहे हो?	Are you not hearing?
10.	क्या वे नहीं बजा रहे है?	Are they not playing on?
11.	क्या लड़के नहीं हंस रहे है?	Are the boys not laughing?
12.	क्या लड़कियाँ फूल नहीं सूंघ रही है?	Are the girls not smelling the flowers?

28th Day

5. Interrogative Positive Sentences:- {with Question words}

आलोक– What – क्या, When – कब, Where – कहाँ, How – कैसे, Why – क्यों, Who – कौन, Which – किसे, Whom – किसको।

1.	वह क्यों जा रहा है?	Why is he going?
2.	वह क्या खा रही है?	What is she eating?
3.	राम क्या पढ़ रहा है?	What is Ram reading?
4.	सीता कैसे खेल रही है?	How is Sita playing?
5.	लड़का कहां दौड़ रहा है?	Where is the boy running?
6.	लड़की क्या गा रही है?	What is the girl singing?
7.	मैं कब आ रहा हूँ?	When am I coming?
8.	हम क्यों जा रहे है?	Why are we going?
9.	तुम क्या सुन रहे हो?	What are you hearing?
10.	वे क्या बजा रहे है?	What are they playing on?
11.	लड़के क्यों हंस रहे है?	Why are the boys laughing?
12.	लड़कियाँ कैसे देख रही है?	How are the girls looking?

6. Interrogative Negative Sentences:- {with Question words}

1.	वह कहां नहीं जा रहा है?	Where is he not going?
2.	वह क्या नहीं खा रही है?	What is she not eating?
3.	राम क्यों नहीं पढ़ रहा है?	Why is Ram not reading?
4.	सीता कब नहीं खेल रही है?	When is Sita not playing?
5.	लड़का क्यों नहीं दौड़ रहा है?	Why is the boy not running?

6. लड़की क्या नहीं गा रही है? What is the girl not singing?
7. मैं वहां क्यों नहीं आ रहा हूँ? Why am I not coming here?
8. हम क्या नहीं नहा रहे है? What are we not taking bath?
9. तुम क्या नहीं सुन रहे हो? What are you not hearing?
10. वे क्या नहीं बजा रहे है? What are they not playing on?
11. लड़के कब नहीं हंस रहे है? When are the boys not laughing?
12. लड़कियाँ क्यों नहीं देख रही है? Why are the girls not looking?

29th Day

5 – Past Continuous / Imperfect / Progressive Tense

1. Positive Sentences:-

1. वह जा रहा था।	He was going.
2. वह खा रही थी।	She was eating.
3. राम पढ़ रहा था।	Ram was reading.
4. सीता खेल रही थी।	Sita was playing.
5. लड़का दौड़ रहा था।	The boy was running.
6. लड़की गा रही थी।	The girl was singing.
7. मैं आ रहा था।	I was coming.
8. हम नहा रहे थे।	We were bathing.
9. तुम सुन रहे थे।	You were hearing.
10. वे बजा रहे थे।	They were playing on.
11. लड़के हंस रहे थे।	The boys were laughing.
12. लड़कियाँ देख रही थी।	The girls were looking.

2. Negative Sentences:-

1. वह नहीं जा रहा था।	He was not going.
2. वह नहीं खा रही थी।	She was not eating.
3. राम नहीं पढ़ रहा था।	Ram was not reading.
4. सीता नहीं खेल रही थी।	Sita was not playing.
5. लड़का नहीं दौड़ रहा था।	The boy was not running.

6.	लड़की नहीं गा रही थी।	The girl was not singing.
7.	मैं नहीं आ रहा था।	I was not coming.
8.	हम नहीं नहा रहे थे।	We were not bathing.
9.	तुम नहीं सुन रहे थे।	You were not hearing.
10.	वे नहीं बजा रहे थे।	They were not playing on.
11.	लड़के नहीं हंस रहे थे।	The boys were not laughing.
12.	लड़कियाँ नहीं देख रही थी।	The girls were not looking.

30th Day

3. Interrogative Positive Sentences:-

1.	क्या वह जा रहा था?	Was he going?
2.	क्या वह खा रही थी?	Was she eating?
3.	क्या राम पढ़ रहा था?	Was Ram reading?
4.	क्या सीता खेल रही थी?	Was Sita playing?
5.	क्या लड़का दौड रहा था?	Was the boy running?
6.	क्या लड़की गा रही थी?	Was the girl singing?
7.	क्या मैं आ रहा था?	Was I coming?
8.	क्या हम नहा रहे थे?	Were we bathing?
9.	क्या तुम सुन रहे थे?	Were you hearing?
10.	क्या वे बजा रहे थे?	Were they playing on?
11.	क्या लड़के हंस रहे थे?	Were the boys laughing?
12.	क्या लड़कियाँ देख रही थी?	Were the girls looking?

4. Interrogative Negative Sentences:-

1.	क्या वह नहीं जा रहा था?	Was he not going?
2.	क्या वह नहीं खा रही थी?	Was she not eating?
3.	क्या राम नहीं पढ़ रहा था?	Was Ram not reading?
4.	क्या सीता नहीं खेल रही थी?	Was Sita not playing?
5.	क्या लड़का नहीं दौड़ रहा था?	Was the boy not running?
6.	क्या लड़की नहीं गा रही थी?	Was the girl not singing?

7. क्या मैं नहीं आ रहा था? Was I not coming?
8. क्या हम नहीं नहा रहे थे? Were we not bathing?
9. क्या तुम नहीं सुन रहे थे? Were you not hearing?
10. क्या वे नहीं बजा रहे थे? Were they not playing on?
11. क्या लड़के नहीं हंस रहे थे? Were the boys not laughing?
12. क्या लड़कियाँ नहीं देख रही थी? Were the girls not looking?

31th Day

5. Interrogative Positive Sentences:- {with Question words}

आलोक– What – क्या, When – कब, Where – कहाँ, How – कैसे, Why – क्यों, Who – कौन, Which – किसे, Whom – किसको।

1. वह कहां जा रहा था?	Where was he going?
2. वह क्या खा रही थी?	What was she eating?
3. राम पत्र कब पढ़ रहा था?	When was Ram reading letter?
4. सीता क्या खेल रही थी?	What was Sita playing?
5. लड़का कहां दौड़ रहा था?	Where was the boy running?
6. सुषमा गाना कब गा रही थी?	When was Sushma singing a song?
7. मैं वहां क्या कर रहा था?	What was I doing there?
8. हम कहां नहा रहे थे?	Where were we bathing?
9. तुम क्या सुन रहे थे?	What were you hearing?
10. वे क्या बजा रहे थे?	What were they playing on?
11. लड़के क्यों हंस रहे थे?	Why were the boys laughing?
12. लड़कियाँ क्या देख रही थी?	What were the girls looking?

6. Interrogative Negative Sentences:- {with Question words}

1. वह घर क्यों नहीं जा रहा था?	Why was he not going to home?
2. वह रोटी क्यों नहीं खा रही थी?	Why was she not eating the bread?

3. राम कब नहीं पढ़ रहा था?	When was Ram not reading?
4. सीता हॉकी क्यों नहीं खेल रही थी?	Why was Sita not playing hockey?
5. लड़का क्यों नहीं दौड़ रहा था?	Why was the boy not running?
6. राधिका क्या नहीं गा रही थी?	What was the Radhika not singing?
7. मैं क्येां नहीं आ रहा था?	Why was I not coming?
8. हम कब नहीं नहा रहे थे?	When were we not taking bath?
9. तुम क्या नहीं सुन रहे थे?	What were you not hearing?
10. वे क्या नहीं बजा रहे थे?	What were they not playing on?
11. लड़के क्यों नहीं हंस रहे थे?	Why were the boys not laughing?
12. लड़कियाँ क्या नहीं देख रही थी?	What were the girls not looking?

32nd Day

6. Future Continuous / Imperfect / Progressive Tense

1. Positive Sentences:-

1. वह जा रहा होगा।	He will be going.
2. वह खा रही होगी।	She will be eating.
3. राम पढ़ रहा होगा।	Ram will be reading.
4. सीता खेल रही होगी।	Sita will be playing.
5. लड़का दौड़ रहा होगा।	The boy will be running.
6. लड़की गा रही होगी।	The girl will be singing.
7. मैं आता रहूंगा।	I shall be coming.
8. हम नहा रहे होगें।	We shall be taking bath.
9. तुम सुन रहे होगें।	You will be hearing.
10. वे बजा रहे होगें।	They will be playing on.
11. लड़के हँस रहे होगें।	The boys will be laughing.
12. लड़कियाँ देख रही होगीं।	The girls will be looking.

2. Negative Sentences:-

1. वह नहीं जा रहा होगा।	He will not be going.
2. वह नहीं खा रही होगी।	She will not be eating.
3. राम नहीं पढ़ रहा होगा।	Ram will not be reading.
4. सीता नहीं खेल रही होगी।	Sita will not be playing.
5. लड़का नहीं दौड़ रहा होगा।	The boy will not be running.

6. लड़की नहीं गा रही होगी।	The girl will not be singing.
7. मैं नहीं आ रहा हूंगा।	I shall not be coming.
8. हम नहीं नहा रहे होंगे।	We shall not be taking bath.
9. तुम नहीं सुन रहे होंगे।	You will not be hearing.
10. वे नहीं बजा रहे होंगे।	They will not be playing on.
11. लड़के नहीं हंस रहे होंगे।	The boys will not be laughing.
12. लड़कियाँ नहीं देख रही थी।	The girls will not be looking.

33th Day

3. Interrogative Positive Sentences:-

1.	क्या वह जा रहा होगा?	Will he be going?
2.	क्या वह खा रही होगी?	Will she be eating?
3.	क्या राम पढ़ रहा होगा?	Will Ram be reading?
4.	क्या सीता खेल रही होगी?	Will Sita be playing?
5.	क्या लड़का दौड रहा होगा?	Will the boy be running?
6.	क्या लड़की गा रही होगी?	Will the girl be singing?
7.	क्या मैं आता रहूँगा?	Shall I be coming?
8.	क्या हम नहाते रहोगे?	Shall we be taking bath?
9.	क्या तुम सुन रहे होंगे?	Will you be hearing?
10.	क्या वे बजा रहे होंगे?	Will they be playing on?
11.	क्या लड़के हंस रहे होंगे?	Will the boys be laughing?
12.	क्या लड़कियाँ देख रही होगी?	Will the girls be looking?

4. Interrogative Negative Sentences:-

1.	क्या वह नहीं जा रहा होगा?	Will he not be going?
2.	क्या वह नहीं खा रही होगी?	Will she not be eating?
3.	क्या राम नहीं पढ़ रहा होगा?	Will Ram not be reading?
4.	क्या सीता नहीं खेल रही होगी?	Will Sita not be playing?
5.	क्या लड़का नहीं दौड़ रहा होगा?	Will the boy not be running?
6.	क्या लड़की नहीं गा रही होगी?	Will the girl not be singing?

7.	क्या मैं नहीं आता रहूँगा?	Shall I not be coming?
8.	क्या हम नहीं नहाते रहेंगे?	Shall we not be taking bath?
9.	क्या तुम नहीं सुनते रहेंगे?	Will you not be hearing?
10.	क्या वे नहीं बजा रहे होंगे?	Will they not be playing on?
11.	क्या लड़के नहीं हंस रहे होंगे?	Will the boys not be laughing?
12.	क्या लड़कियाँ नहीं देख रही होंगी?	Will the girls not be looking?

34th Day

5. **Interrogative Positive Sentences:- {with Question words}**

आलोक– What – क्या, When – कब, Where – कहाँ, How – कैसे, Why – क्यों, Who – कौन, Which – किसे, Whom – किसको।

1. वह कहां जा रहा होगा? Where will he be going?
2. वह क्या खा रही होगी? What will she be eating?
3. राम क्या पढ़ रहा होगा? What will Ram be reading?
4. सीता क्या खेल रही होगी? What will Sita be playing?
5. लड़का क्यों दौड़ रहा होगा? Why will the boy be running?
6. लड़की कब गा रही होगी? When will the girl be singing?
7. मैं तुम्हारे घर क्यों आता रहूँगा? Why shall I be coming at your home?
8. हम कब नहा रहे होंगे? When shall we be taking bath?
9. तुम क्या सुन रहे होंगे? What will you be hearing?
10. वे क्या बजा रहे होंगे? What will they be playing on?
11. लड़के तुम पर क्यों हंस रहे होंगे? Why will the boys be laughing on you?
12. लड़कियाँ क्या देख रही होगी? What will the girls be looking?

6. **Interrogative Negative Sentences:- {with Question words}**

1. वह कहां नहीं जा रहा होगा? Where will he not be going?

2. वह क्या नहीं खा रही होगी? What will she not be eating?
3. राम अंग्रेजी क्यों नहीं पढ़ रहा होगा? Why will Ram not be reading English?
4. सीता क्या नहीं खेल रही होगी? What will Sita not be playing?
5. लड़का नदी में क्यों नहीं कूद रहा होगा? Why will the boy not be jumping into the river?
6. लड़की क्या नहीं गा रही होगी? What will the girl not be singing?
7. मैं कब नहीं आ रहा होगा? When shall I not be coming?
8. हम कैसे नहीं नहा रहे होंगे? How shall we not be taking bath?
9. तुम क्या नहीं सुनते रहोगे? What will you not be hearing?
10. वे क्या नहीं बजा रहे होंगे? What will they not be playing on?
11. लड़के क्यों नहीं रो रहे होंगे? Why will the boys not be weeping?
12. लड़कियाँ क्या नहीं देख रही होगी? What will the girls not be looking?

35th Day

7. Present Perfect Tense

Rule:-Subject + has / have + verb 3rd form + object + other words.

1. **Positive Sentences:-**

1.	वह जा चुका है।	He has gone.
2.	वह खा चुकी है।	She has eaten.
3.	राम पढ़ चुका है।	Ram has read.
4.	सीता खेल चुकी है।	Sita has played.
5.	लड़का दौड़ा है।	The boy has run.
6.	लड़की गाया है।	The girl has sung.
7.	मैं आ चुका हूँ।	I have come.
8.	हम नहाये है।	We have taken bath.
9.	तुम सुन चुके है।	You have heard.
10.	वे बजा चुके है।	They have played on.
11.	लड़के हंसे है।	The boys have laughed.
12.	लड़कियाँ देख चुकी है।	The girls have looked.

2. **Negative Sentences:-**

1.	वह नहीं जा चुका है।	He has not gone.
2.	वह नहीं खा चुकी है।	She has not eaten.
3.	राम नहीं पढ़ चुका है।	Ram has not read.
4.	सीता नहीं खेल चुकी है।	Sita has not played.

5.	लड़का नहीं दौड़ा है।	The boy has not run.
6.	लड़की ने नहीं गाया है।	The girl has not sung.
7.	मैं नहीं आ चुका हूँ।	I have not come.
8.	हम नहीं नहाये है।	We have not taken bath.
9.	तुम नहीं सुन चुके है।	You have not heard.
10.	वे नहीं बजा चुके है।	They have not played on.
11.	लड़के नहीं हंसे है।	The boys have not laughed.
12.	लड़कियाँ नहीं देख चुकी है।	The girls have not looked.

36th Day

3. Interrogative Positive Sentences:-

1. क्या वह जा चुका है?	Has he gone?
2. क्या वह खा चुकी है?	Has she eaten?
3. क्या राम पढ़ चुका है?	Has Ram read?
4. क्या सीता खेल चुकी है?	Has Sita played?
5. क्या लड़का दौड़ा है?	Has the boy run?
6. क्या लड़की ने गाया है?	Has the girl sung?
7. क्या मैं आ चुका हूँ?	Have I come?
8. क्या हम नहाये है?	Have we taken bath?
9. क्या तुम सुन चुके है?	Have you heard?
10. क्या वे बजा चुके है?	Have they played on?
11. क्या लड़के हंसे है?	Have the boys laughed?
12. क्या लड़कियाँ देख चुकी है?	Have the girls looked?

4. Interrogative Negative Sentences:-

1. क्या वह नहीं जा चुका है?	Has he not gone?
2. क्या वह नहीं खा चुकी है?	Has she not eaten?
3. क्या राम नहीं पढ़ चुका है?	Has Ram not read?
4. क्या सीता नहीं खेल चुकी है?	Has Sita not played?
5. क्या लड़का नहीं दौड़ा है?	Has the boy not run?
6. क्या लड़की ने नहीं गाया है?	Has the girl not sung?

7.	क्या मैं नहीं आ चुका हूँ?	Have I not come?
8.	क्या हम नहीं नहाये है?	Have we not taken bath?
9.	क्या तुम नहीं सुन चुके है?	Have you not heard?
10.	क्या वे नहीं बजा चुके है?	Have they not played on?
11.	क्या लड़के नहीं हंसे है?	Have the boys not laughed?
12.	क्या लड़कियाँ नहीं देख चुकी है?	Have the girls not looked?

37th Day

5. Interrogative Positive Sentences:- {with Question words}

आलोक– What – क्या, When – कब, Where – कहाँ, How – कैसे, Why – क्यों, Who – कौन, Which – किसे, Whom – किसको।

1.	वह वहां से क्यों जा चुका है?	Why has he gone from there?
2.	वह कब खा चुकी है?	When has she eaten?
3.	राम क्या पढ़ चुका है?	What has Ram read?
4.	सीता क्या खेल चुकी है?	What has Sita played?
5.	लड़का क्या दौड़ा है?	What has the boy run?
6.	लड़की ने क्या गाया है?	What has the girl sung?
7.	मैं कहां आ चुका हूँ?	Where have I come?
8.	हम क्यों नहाये है?	Why have we taken bath?
9.	तुम क्या सुन चुके हो?	What have you heard?
10.	वे क्या बजा चुके है?	What have they played on?
11.	लड़के तुम पर क्यों हंसे है?	Why have the boys laughed on you?
12.	लड़कियाँ क्या देख चुकी है?	What have the girls looked?

6. Interrogative Negative Sentences:- {with Question words}

1.	वह कहां नहीं जा चुका है?	Where has he not gone?
2.	वह क्या नहीं खा चुकी है?	What has she not eaten?
3.	राम क्या नहीं पढ़ चुका है?	What has Ram not read?

4.	सीता क्या नहीं खेल चुकी है?	What has Sita not played?
5.	लड़का क्यों नहीं दौड़ा है?	Why has the boy not run?
6.	लड़की ने क्या नहीं गाया है?	What has the girl not sung?
7.	मैं क्या नहीं आ चुका हूँ?	Why have I not come?
8.	हम कैसे नहीं नहाये है?	When have we not taken bath?
9.	तुम क्या नहीं सुन चुके हो?	What have you not heard?
10.	वे क्या नहीं बजा चुके है?	What have they not played on?
11.	लड़के उस पर क्यों नहीं हंसे है?	What have the boys not laughed on him?
12.	लड़कियाँ क्या नहीं देख चुकी है?	What have the girls not looked?

38th Day

8. Past Perfect Tense

Rule:- Subject + had + verb 3rd form + object + other words.

1. Positive Sentences:-

1.	वह जा चुका था।	He had gone.
2.	वह पहले ही खा चुकी थी।	She had already eaten.
3.	राम कल तक पढ़ चुका था।	Ram had read till yesterday.
4.	सीता ने आज तक खेला था।	Sita had played till today.
5.	लड़का पहले ही दौड़ा चुका था।	The boy had already run.
6.	लड़की गा चुकी थी।	The girl had sung.
7.	मैं आया था।	I had come.
8.	हम नहाये थे।	We had taken bath.
9.	तुम सुन चुके थे।	You had heard.
10.	वे बजा चुके थे।	They had played.
11.	मेरे हंसने के बाद लड़के हंसे थे।	The boys had laughed after I laughed.
12.	हमारे देखने से पहले लड़कियाँ देख चुकी थी।	The girls had looked before we looked.

2. Negative Sentences:-

1.	वह नहीं जा चुका था।	He had not gone.
2.	वह पहले नहीं खा चुकी थी।	She had not eaten already.

3. राम कल तक नहीं पढ़ चुका था।	Ram had not read till yesterday.
4. सीता ने आज तक नहीं खेला था।	Sita had not played till today.
5. लड़का पहले नहीं दौड़ा था।	The boy had not already run.
6. लड़की नहीं गा चुकी थी।	The girl had not sung.
7. मैं नहीं आया था।	I had not come.
8. हम नहीं नहाये थे।	We had not taken bath.
9. तुम नहीं सुन चुके थे।	You had not heard.
10. वे नहीं बजा चुके थे।	They had not played on.
11. मेरे हँसने के बाद लड़के नहीं हँसे थे।	The boys had not laughed after I laughed.
12. हमारे देखने से पहले लड़कियाँ नहीं देख चुकी थी।	The girls had not looked before we looked.

39th Day

3. Interrogative Positive Sentences:-

1.	क्या वह जा चुका था?	Had he gone?
2.	क्या वह खा चुकी थी?	Had she eaten?
3.	क्या राम पढ़ चुका था?	Had Ram read?
4.	क्या सीता खेल चुकी थी?	Had Sita played?
5.	क्या लड़का दौड़ा था?	Had the boy run?
6.	क्या लड़की ने गाया था?	Had the girl sung?
7.	क्या मैं पहले ही आ चुका था?	Had I already come?
8.	क्या हम नहाये थे?	Had we taken bath?
9.	क्या तुम कल तक सुन चुके थे?	Had you heard till yesterday?
10.	क्या वे बजा चुके थे?	Had they played?
11.	मेरे आने से पूर्व क्या लड़के हँस चुके थे?	Had the boys laughed before I come?
12.	क्या लड़कियाँ देख चुकी थी?	Had the girls looked?

4. Interrogative Negative Sentences:-

1.	क्या वह नहीं जा चुका था?	Had he not gone?
2.	क्या वह नहीं खा चुकी थी?	Had she not eaten?
3.	क्या राम नहीं पढ़ चुका था?	Had Ram not read?
4.	क्या सीता नहीं खेल चुकी थी?	Had Sita not played?
5.	क्या लड़का नहीं दौड़ा था?	Had the boy not run?

6.	क्या लड़की नहीं गाया था?	Had the girl not sung?
7.	क्या मैं पहले ही नहीं आ चुका था?	Had I not already come?
8.	क्या हम नहीं नहाये थे?	Had we not taken bath?
9.	क्या तुम कल तक नहीं सुन चुके थे?	Had you not heard till yesterday?
10.	क्या वे नहीं बजा चुके थे?	Had they not played?
11.	क्या लड़के नहीं हँसे चुके थे?	Had the boys not laughed?
12.	मेरे आने से पूर्व क्या लड़कियाँ नहीं देख चुकी थी?	Had the girls not looked before I come?

40th Day

5. **Interrogative Positive Sentences:- {with Question words}**

आलोक– What – क्या, When – कब, Where – कहाँ, How – कैसे, Why – क्यों, Who – कौन, Which – किसे, Whom – किसको।

1.	वह कहाँ जा चुका था?	Where had he gone?
2.	वह क्या खा चुकी थी?	What had she eaten?
3.	राम पत्र कब पढ़ चुका था?	When had Ram read a letter?
4.	सीता क्या खेल चुकी थी?	What had Sita played?
5.	लड़का क्यों दौड़ा था?	Why had the boy run?
6.	लड़की ने क्या गाया था?	What had the girl sung?
7.	मैं क्या पहले ही आ चुका था?	What had I already come?
8.	हम कैसे नहाये थे?	How had we taken bath?
9.	तुम कल तक क्या सुन चुके थे?	What had you heard till yesterday?
10.	वे क्या बजा चुके थे?	What had they played ?
11.	लड़के क्यों हंस चुके थे?	Why had the boys laughed?
12.	मेरे आने से पूर्व लड़कियाँ क्या देख चुकी थी?	What had the girls looked before I come?

6. **Interrogative Negative Sentences:- {with Question words}**

1.	वह क्यों नहीं जा चुका था?	Why had he not gone?
2.	वह क्या नहीं खा चुकी थी?	What had she not eaten?

3.	राम कब नहीं पढ़ चुका था?	When had Ram not read?
4.	सीता क्या नहीं खेल चुकी थी?	What had Sita not played?
5.	लड़का कब नहीं दौड़ा था?	When had the boy not run?
6.	लड़की ने क्या नहीं गाया था?	What had the girl not sung?
7.	मैं पहले ही क्यों नहीं आ चुका था?	Why had I not already come?
8.	हम कैसे नहीं नहाये थे?	How had we not taken bath?
9.	तुम कल तक क्या नहीं सुन चुके थे?	What had you not heard till yesterday?
10.	वे क्या नहीं बजा चुके थे?	What had they not played?
11.	लड़के क्यों नहीं हंस चुके थे?	Why had the boys not laughed?
12.	मेरे आने से पूर्व लड़कियाँ किसे नहीं देख चुकी थी?	Whom had the girls not looked before I come?

41st Day

9. Future Perfect Tense

Rule:- Subject + will have / shall have + verb 3rd form + object + other words.

1. **Positive Sentences:-**

1.	वह जा चुका होगा।	He will have gone.
2.	वह खा चुकी होगी।	She will have eaten.
3.	राम पढ़ चुका होगा।	Ram will have read.
4.	सीता खेल चुकी होगी।	Sita will have played.
5.	लड़का दौड़ चुका होगा।	The boy will have run.
6.	लड़की गा चुकी होगी।	The girl will have sung.
7.	मैं आ चुका हूंगा।	I shall have come.
8.	हम नहा चुके होगें।	We shall have taken bath.
9.	तुम सुन चुके होगें।	You will have heard.
10.	वे सोमवार तक बजा चुके होगें।	They will have played by monday.
11.	लड़के हँस चुके होगें।	The boys will have laughed.
12.	लड़को के आने से पहले लड़कियाँ देख चुकी होगीं।	The girls will have looked before the boys come.

2. **Negative Sentences:-**

1.	वह नहीं जा चुका होगा।	He will not have gone.
2.	वह नहीं खा चुकी होगी।	She will not have eaten.

3.	राम नहीं पढ़ चुका होगा।	Ram will not have read.
4.	सीता कल तक नहीं खेल चुकी होगी।	Sita will not have played by tommorow.
5.	लड़का नहीं दौड़ चुका होगा।	The boy will not have run.
6.	लड़की ने नहीं गाया होगा।	The girl will not have sung.
7.	मैं नहीं आ चुकूँगा	I shall not have come.
8.	हम नहीं नहा चुके होंगे।	We shall not have taken bath.
9.	तुम नहीं सुन चुके होंगे।	You will not have heard.
10.	वे सोमवार तक नहीं बजा चुके होंगे।	They will not have played by monday.
11.	लड़के नहीं हँस चुके होंगे।	The boys will not have laughed.
12.	लड़को के आने से पहले लड़कियाँ नहीं देख चुकी होंगी।	The girls will not have looked before the boys come.

42nd Day

3. Interrogative Positive Sentences:-

1. क्या वह जा चुका होगा?	Will he have gone?
2. क्या वह खा चुकी होगी?	Will she have eaten?
3. क्या राम पढ़ चुका होगा?	Will Ram have read?
4. क्या सीता खेल चुकी होगी?	Will Sita have played?
5. क्या लड़का दौड़ चुकेगा?	Will the boy have run?
6. क्या लड़की ने गाया होगा?	Will the girl have sung?
7. क्या मैं आ चुकूँगा?	Shall I have come?
8. क्या हम नहा चुके होंगे?	Shall we have taken bath?
9. क्या तुम सुन चुके होंगे?	Will you have heard?
10. क्या वे सोमवार तक बजा चुके होंगे?	Will they have played by monday?
11. क्या लड़के हँस चुके होंगे?	Will the boys have laughed?
12. क्या लड़को के आने से पूर्व लड़कियाँ देख चुकी होगी?	Will the girls have looked before the boys come?

4. Interrogative Negative Sentences:-

1. क्या वह नहीं जा चुका होगा?	Will he not have gone?
2. क्या वह नहीं खा चुकी होगी?	Will she not have eaten?
3. क्या राम नहीं पढ़ चुका होगा?	Will Ram not have read?
4. क्या सीता कल तक नहीं खेल चुकी होगी?	Will Sita not have played by tommorow?

5.	क्या लड़का नहीं दौड़ चुकेगा होगा?	Will the boy not have run?
6.	क्या लड़की ने नहीं गाया होगा?	Will the girl not have sung?
7.	क्या मैं नहीं आ चुकूँगा?	Shall I not have come?
8.	क्या हम नहीं नहा चुकेगे?	Shall we not have taken bath?
9.	क्या तुम नहीं सुन चुके होंगे?	Will you not have heard?
10.	क्या वे सोमवार तक नहीं बजा चुके होंगे?	Will they not have played by Monday?
11.	क्या लड़के नहीं हंस चुके होंगे?	Will the boys not have laughed?
12.	क्या लड़कों के आने से पूर्व लड़कियाँ नहीं देख चुकी होगी?	Will the girls not have looked before the boys come?

43rd Day

5. Interrogative Positive Sentences:- {with Question words}

आलोक– What – क्या, When – कब, Where – कहाँ, How – कैसे, Why – क्यों, Who – कौन, Which – किसे, Whom – किसको।

1. वह कहां जा चुका होगा?	Where will he have gone?
2. वह क्या खा चुकी होगी?	What will she have eaten?
3. राम क्या पढ़ चुका होगा?	What will Ram have read?
4. सीता कब खेल चुकी होगी?	When will Sita have played?
5. लड़का कहां दौड़ चुका होगा?	Where will the boy have run?
6. लड़की क्या गा चुकी होगी?	What will the girl have sung?
7. मैं कब आ चुका होगा?	When shall I have come?
8. हम क्यों नहा चुके होंगे?	Why shall we have taken bath?
9. तुम क्या सुन चुके होंगे?	What will you have heard?
10. वे कल तक क्या बजा चुके होंगे?	What will they have played by tommorow?
11. लड़के तब क्यों हंसे होंगे?	Why will the boys have laughed then?
12. लड़को के आने से पूर्व लड़कियाँ क्या देख चुकी होगी?	What will the girls have looked before the boys come?

6. Interrogative Negative Sentences:- {with Question words}

1. वह क्यों नहीं जा चुका होगा?	Why will he not have gone?
2. वह क्या नहीं खा चुकी होगी?	What will she not have eaten?

3. राम क्या नहीं पढ़ चुका होगा?	What will Ram not have read?
4. सीता क्या नहीं खेल चुकी होगी?	What will Sita not have played?
5. लड़का क्यों नहीं दौड़ चुका होगा?	Why will the boy not have run?
6. लड़की क्या नहीं गा चुकी होगी?	What will the girl not have sung?
7. मैं कब नहीं आ चुका होगा?	When shall I not have come?
8. हम कैसे नहीं नहा चुके होंगे?	How shall we not have taken bath?
9. तुम क्या नहीं सुन चुके होंगे?	What will you not have heard?
10. वे क्या कल तक नहीं बजा चुके होंगे?	What will they not have played by tommorow?
11. लड़के क्यों नहीं हँसे होंगे?	Why will the boys not have laughed?
12. लड़कों के आने के बाद लड़कियाँ क्या नहीं देख चुकी होंगी?	What will the girls not have looked after the boys come?

44th Day

10. Present Perfect Continuous Tense

Rule:- Subject + has been / have been + verb 1st form + ing + object + other words + since (appoint of time) + for (Period of time) + tense.

1. **Positive Sentences:-**

1. वह सुबह से जा रहा है।
   He has been going since morning.
2. वह दो बजे से खा रही है।
   She has been eating since 2 o' clock.
3. राम रात्रि से पढ़ रहा है।
   Ram has been reading since night.
4. सीता दोपहर से खेल रही है।
   Sita has been playing since noon.
5. लड़का सोमवार से दौड़ रहा है।
   The boy has been running since Monday.
6. लड़की जुलाई से गा रही है।
   The girl has been singing since July.
7. मैं दो दिन से आ रहा हूँ।
   I have been coming for 2 days.
8. हम दो सप्ताह से नहा रहे है।
   We have been taking bath for 2 weeks.
9. तुम दो माह से सुन रहे हो।
   You have been hearing for 2 months.

10. वे कल से बजा रहे है।
    They have been playing on since yesterday.
11. लड़के दो वर्ष से हंस रहे है।
    The boys have been laughing for 2 years.
12. लड़कियाँ दो घण्टे से देख रही हैं।
    The girls have been looking for 2 hours.

2. Negative Sentences:-

1. वह सुबह से नहीं जा रहा है।
   He has not been going since morning.
2. वह दो बजे से नहीं खा रही है।
   She has not been eating since 2 o' clock.
3. राम रात्रि से नहीं पढ़ रहा है।
   Ram has not been reading since night.
4. सीता दोपहर से नहीं खेल रही है।
   Sita has not been playing since noon.
5. लड़का सोमवार से नहीं दौड़ रहा है।
   The boy has not been running since Monday.
6. लड़की जुलाई से नहीं गा रही है।
   The girl has not been singing since July.
7. मैं दो दिन से नहीं आ रहा हूँ।
   I have not been coming for 2 days.
8. हम दो सप्ताह से नहीं नहा रहे हैं।
   We have not been taking bath for 2 weeks.
9. तुम दो माह से नहीं सुन रहे हो।
   You have not been hearing for 2 months.
10. वे कल से नहीं बजा रहे है।
    They have not been playing on since yesterday.
11. लड़के दो वर्ष से नहीं हंस रहे है।
    The boys have not been laughing for 2 years.
12. लड़कियाँ दो घण्टे से नहीं देख रही है।
    The girls have not been looking for 2 hours.

45th Day

3. Interrogative Positive Sentences:-

1. क्या वह सुबह से जा रहा है?
   Has he been going since morning?
2. क्या वह दो बजे से खा रही है?
   Has she been eating since 2 o' clock?
3. क्या राम रात्रि से पढ़ रहा है?
   Has Ram been reading since night?
4. क्या सीता दोपहर से खेल रही है?
   Has Sita been playing since noon?
5. क्या लड़का सोमवार से दौड़ रहा है?
   Has the boy been running since Monday?
6. क्या लड़की जुलाई से गा रही है?
   Has the girl been singing since July?
7. क्या मैं दो दिन से आ रहा हूँ?
   Have I been coming for 2 days?
8. क्या हम दो सप्ताह से नहा रहे हैं?
   Have we been taking bath for 2 weeks?
9. क्या तुम दो माह से सुन रहे हो?
   Have you been hearing for 2 months?
10. क्या वे कल से बजा रहे है?
    Have they been playing on since yesterday?
11. क्या लड़के दो वर्ष से हंस रहे है?
    Have the boys been laughing for 2 years?

12. क्या लड़कियाँ दो घण्टे से देख रही है?
    Have the girls been looking for 2 hours?

4. **Interrogative Negative Sentences:-**

1. क्या वह सुबह से नहीं जा रहा है?
   Has he not been going since morning?
2. क्या वह दो बजे से नहीं खा रही है?
   Has she not been eating since 2 o' clock?
3. क्या राम रात्रि से नहीं पढ़ रहा है?
   Has Ram not been reading since night?
4. क्या सीता दोपहर से नहीं खेल रही है?
   Has Sita not been playing since noon?
5. क्या लड़का सोमवार से नहीं दौड़ रहा है?
   Has the boy not been running since Monday?
6. क्या लड़की जुलाई से नहीं गा रही है?
   Has the girl not been singing since July?
7. क्या मैं दो दिन से नहीं आ रहा हूँ?
   Have I not been coming for 2 days?
8. क्या हम दो सप्ताह से नहीं नहा रहे है?
   Have we not been taking bath for 2 weeks?
9. क्या तुम दो माह से नहीं सुन रहे हो?
   Have you not been hearing for 2 months?
10. क्या वे कल से नहीं बजा रहे है?
    Have they not been playing on since yesterday?
11. क्या लड़के दो वर्ष से नहीं हंस रहे है?
    Have the boys not been laughing for 2 years?
12. क्या लड़कियाँ दो घण्टे से नहीं देख रही है?
    Have the girls not been looking for 2 hours?

46th Day

5. Interrogative Positive Sentences:- {with Question words}

आलोक– What – क्या, When – कब, Where – कहाँ, How – कैसे, Why – क्यों, Who – कौन, Which – किसे, Whom – किसको।

1. वह सुबह से कहाँ जा रहा है?
   Where has he been going since morning?
2. वह दो बजे से क्या खा रही है?
   What has she been eating since 2 o' clock?
3. राम क्या रात्रि से पढ़ रहा है?
   What has Ram been reading since night?
4. सीता दोपहर से क्या खेल रही है?
   What has Sita been playing since noon?
5. लड़का सोमवार से क्यों दौड़ रहा है?
   Why has the boy been running since Monday?
6. लड़की जुलाई से क्या गा रही है?
   What has the girl been singing since July?
7. मैं दो दिन से कहां जा रहा हूँ?
   Where have I been going for 2 days?
8. मैं दो सप्ताह से कब नहा रहा हूँ?
   When have I been taking bath for 2 weeks?
9. तुम दो माह से क्या सुन रहे हो?
   What have you been hearing for 2 months?
10. वे कल से बांसुरी क्यों बजा रहे है?
    Why have they been blowing flute since yesterday?

11. लड़के दो वर्ष से कहां हँस रहे है?
    Where have the boys been laughing for 2 years?
12. लड़कियाँ क्या दो घण्टे से देख रही है?
    What have the girls been looking for 2 hours?

6. Interrogative negative sentences/ with question words.

1. वह सुबह से कहां नहीं जा रहा है?
   Where has he not been going since morning?
2. वह दो बजे से क्या नहीं खा रही है?
   What has she not been eating since 2 o' clock?
3. राम रात्रि से क्यों नहीं पढ़ रहा है?
   Why has Ram not been reading since night?
4. सीता दोपहर से क्या नहीं खेल रही है?
   What has Sita not been playing since noon?
5. लड़का सोमवार से क्यों नहीं दौड़ रहा है?
   Why has the boy not been running since Monday?
6. लड़की जुलाई से क्या नहीं गा रही है?
   What has the girl not been singing since July?
7. मैं दो दिन से कहां नहीं आ रहा हूँ?
   Where have I not been coming for 2 days?
8. हम दो सप्ताह से क्यों नहीं नहा रहे हैं?
   Why have we not been taking bath for 2 weeks?
9. तुम दो माह से क्या नहीं सुन रहे हो?
   What have you not been hearing for 2 months?
10. वे कल से ढोल क्यों नहीं बजा रहे है?
    Why have they not been beating drum since yesterday?
11. लड़के दो वर्ष से क्यों नहीं हंस रहे है?
    Why have the boys not been laughing for 2 years?
12. लड़कियाँ क्या दो घण्टे से नहीं देख रही है?
    What have the girls not been looking for 2 hours?

47th Day

11. Past Perfect Continuous Tense

Rule:- Subject + had been + verb 1st form + ing + object + other words + since (point of time) + for (Period of time) + tense.

1. **Positive Sentences:-**

   1. वह सुबह से जा रहा था।
      He had been going since morning.
   2. वह दो बजे से खा रही थी।
      She had been eating since 2 o' clock.
   3. राम रात्रि से पढ़ रहा था।
      Ram had been reading since night.
   4. सीता दोपहर से खेल रही थी।
      Sita had been playing since noon.
   5. लड़का सोमवार से दौड़ रहा था।
      The boy had been running since Monday.
   6. लड़की जुलाई से गा रही थी।
      The girl had been singing since July.
   7. मैं दो दिन से आ रहा था।
      I had been coming for 2 days.
   8. हम दो सप्ताह से नहा रहे थे।
      We had been taking bath for 2 weeks.
   9. तुम दो माह से सुन रहे थे।
      You had been hearing for 2 months.

10. वे कल से बजा रहे थे।
    They had been playing on since yesterday.
11. लड़के दो वर्ष से हंस रहे थे।
    The boys had been laughing for 2 years.
12. लड़कियाँ दो घण्टे से देख रही थी।
    The girls had been looking for 2 hours.

2. **Negative Sentences:-**
    1. वह सुबह से नहीं जा रहा था।
       He had not been going since morning.
    2. वह दो बजे से नहीं खा रही थी।
       She had not been eating since 2 o' clock.
    3. राम रात्रि से नहीं पढ़ रहा था।
       Ram had not been reading since night.
    4. सीता दोपहर से नहीं खेल रही थी।
       Sita had not been playing since noon.
    5. लड़का सोमवार से नहीं दौड़ रहा था।
       The boy had not been running since Monday.
    6. लड़की जुलाई से नहीं गा रही थी।
       The girl had not been singing since July.
    7. मैं दो दिन से नहीं आ रहा था।
       I had not been coming for 2 days.
    8. हम दो सप्ताह से नहीं नहा रहे थे।
       We had not been taking bath for 2 weeks.
    9. तुम दो माह से नहीं सुन रहे थे।
       You had not been hearing for 2 months.
    10. वे कल से नहीं बजा रहे थे।
        They had not been playing on since yesterday.
    11. लड़के दो वर्ष से नहीं हंस रहे थे।
        The boys had not been laughing for 2 years.
    12. लड़कियाँ दो घण्टे से नहीं देख रही थी।
        The girls had not been looking for 2 hours.

48th Day

3. Interrogative Positive Sentences:-

1. क्या वह सुबह से जा रहा था?
   Had he been going since morning?
2. क्या वह दो बजे से खा रही थी?
   Had she been eating since 2 o' clock?
3. क्या राम रात्रि से पढ़ रहा था?
   Had Ram been reading since night?
4. क्या सीता दोपहर से खेल रही थी?
   Had Sita been playing since noon?
5. क्या लड़का सोमवार से दौड़ रहा था?
   Had the boy been running since Monday?
6. क्या लड़की जुलाई से गा रही थी?
   Had the girl been singing since July?
7. क्या मैं दो दिन से आ रहा था?
   Had I been coming for 2 days?
8. क्या हम दो सप्ताह से नहा रहे थे?
   Had we been taking bath for 2 weeks?
9. क्या तुम दो माह से सुन रहे थे?
   Had you been hearing for 2 months?
10. क्या वे कल से बजा रहे थे?
    Had they been playing on since yesterday?
11. क्या लड़के दो वर्ष से हंस रहे थे?
    Had the boys been laughing for 2 years?

12. क्या लड़कियाँ दो घण्टे से देख रही थी?
    Had the girls been looking for 2 hours?

4. **Interrogative Negative Sentences:-**
    1. क्या वह सुबह से नहीं जा रहा था?
       Had he not been going since morning?
    2. क्या वह दो बजे से नहीं खा रही थी?
       Had she not been eating since 2 o' clock?
    3. क्या राम रात्रि से नहीं पढ़ रहा था?
       Had Ram not been reading since night?
    4. क्या सीता दोपहर से नहीं खेल रही थी?
       Had Sita not been playing since noon?
    5. क्या लड़का सोमवार से नहीं दौड़ रहा था?
       Had the boy not been running since Monday?
    6. क्या लड़की जुलाई से नहीं गा रही थी?
       Had the girl not been singing since July?
    7. क्या मैं दो दिन से नहीं आ रहा था?
       Had I not been coming for 2 days?
    8. क्या हम दो सप्ताह से नहीं नहा रहे थे?
       Had we not been taking bath for 2 weeks?
    9. क्या तुम दो माह से नहीं सुन रहे थे?
       Had you not been hearing for 2 months?
    10. क्या वे कल से नहीं बजा रहे थे?
        Had they not been playing on since yesterday?
    11. क्या लड़के दो वर्ष से नहीं हंस रहे थे?
        Had the boys not been laughing for 2 years?
    12. क्या लड़कियाँ दो घण्टे से नहीं देख रही थी?
        Had the girls not been looking for 2 hours?

49th Day

5. Interrogative Positive Sentences:- {with Question words}

आलोक– What – क्या, When – कब, Where – कहाँ, How – कैसे, Why – क्यों, Who – कौन, Which – किसे, Whom – किसको।

1. वह सुबह से कहां जा रहा था?
   Where had he been going since morning?
2. वह दो बजे से क्या खा रही थी?
   What had she been eating since 2 o' clock?
3. राम रात्रि से कैसे पढ़ रहा था?
   How had Ram been reading since night?
4. सीता दोपहर से क्या खेल रही थी?
   What had Sita been playing since noon?
5. लड़का सोमवार से कब दौड़ रहा था?
   When had the boy been running since Monday?
6. लड़की जुलाई से मन्दिर क्यों जा रही थी?
   Why had the girl been going to temple since July?
7. मैं दो दिन से कहां जा रहा था?
   Where had I been going for 2 days?
8. हम दो सप्ताह से कब नहा रहे थे?
   When had we been taking bath for 2 weeks?
9. तुम दो माह से क्या सुन रहे थे?
   What had you been hearing for 2 months?
10. वे कल से क्या बजा रहे थे?
    What had they been playing on since yesterday?

11. लड़के दो वर्ष से क्यों रों रहे थे?
    Why had the boys been weeping for 2 years?
12. लड़कियाँ दो घण्टे से क्या देख रही थी?
    What had the girls been looking for 2 hours?

6. Interrogative negative sentences/ with question words.

1. वह सुबह से कहां नहीं जा रहा था?
   Where had he not been going since morning?
2. वह दो बजे से क्या नहीं खा रही थी?
   What had she not been eating since 2 o' clock?
3. राम रात्रि से क्यों नहीं पढ़ रहा था?
   Why had Ram not been reading since night?
4. सीता दोपहर से क्या नहीं खेल रही थी?
   What had Sita not been playing since noon?
5. लड़का सोमवार से क्यों नहीं दौड़ रहा था?
   Why had the boy not been running since Monday?
6. लड़की जुलाई से क्या नहीं गा रही थी?
   What had the girl not been singing since July?
7. मैं दो दिन से क्यों नहीं आ रहा था?
   Why had I not been coming for 2 days?
8. हम दो सप्ताह से क्यों नहीं नहा रहे थे?
   Why had we not been taking bath for 2 weeks?
9. तुम दो माह से क्या नहीं सुन रहे थे?
   What had you not been hearing for 2 months?
10. वे कल से क्या नहीं बजा रहे थे?
    What had they not been playing on since yesterday?
11. लड़के दो वर्ष से क्यों नहीं हंस रहे थे?
    Why had the boys not been laughing for 2 years?
12. लड़कियाँ दो घण्टे से क्या नहीं देख रही थी?
    What had the girls not been looking for 2 hours?

50th Day

12. Future Perfect Continuous Tense

Rule:- Subject + will have been / shall have been + verb 1st form + ing + object + other words + since (point of time) + for (Period of time) + tense.

1. **Positive Sentences:-**

1. वह सुबह से शाम तक जा रहा होगा।

   He will have been going <u>from</u> morning <u>to</u> evening.

2. वह दो बजे तक खाती रहेगी।

   She will have been eating <u>till</u> 2 o' clock.

3. राम रात्रि से पढ़ रहा होगा।

   Ram will have been reading <u>since</u> night.

4. सीता दोपहर से खेल रही होगी।

   Sita will have been playing <u>since</u> noon.

5. लड़का सोमवार से दौड़ रहा होगा।

   The boy will have been running <u>since</u> Monday.

6. लड़की जुलाई से गा रही होगी।

   The girl will have been singing <u>since</u> July.

7. मैं दो दिन तक आता रहूँगा।

   I shall have been coming till 2 days.

8. हम दो सप्ताह से नहा रहे होंगे।

   We shall been taking bath for 2 weeks.

9. तुम दो माह से चार माह तक सुनते रहोगे।

   You will have been hearing from 2 months to 4 months.

10. वे कल से बजाते रहेगे।
They will have been playing on since tomorrow.
11. लड़के दो वर्ष से हँस रहे होंगे।
The boys will have been laughing for 2 years.
12. लड़कियाँ दो घण्टे से देख रही होगी।
The girls will have been looking for 2 hours.

2. Negative Sentences:-

1. वह सुबह से शाम तक नहीं जा रहा होगा।
He will not have been going from morning to evening.
2. वह दो बजे तक नहीं खाती रहेगी।
She will not have been eating upto 2 o'clock.
3. राम रात्रि से नहीं पढ़ रहा होगा।
Ram will not have been reading since night.
4. सीता दोपहर से नहीं खेल रही होगी।
Sita will not have been playing since noon.
5. लड़का सोमवार से नहीं दौड़ रहा होगा।
The boy will not have been running since Monday.
6. लड़की जुलाई से नहीं गा रही होगी।
The girl will not have been singing since July.
7. मैं दो दिन से चार दिन तक नहीं आता रहूँगा।
I shall not have been coming from 2 days to 4 days.
8. हम दो सप्ताह से नहीं नहाते रहेंगे।
We shall not have been taking bath till 2 weeks.
9. तुम दो माह से नहीं सुन रहे होंगे।
You will not have been hearing for 2 months.
10. वे कल से नहीं बजा रहे होंगे।
They will not have been playing on since tomorrow.
11. लड़के दो वर्ष से नहीं हंस रहे होंगे।
The boys will not have been laughing for 2 years.
12. लड़कियाँ दो घण्टे से नहीं देख रही होगी।
The girls will not have been looking for 2 hours.

51th Day

3. Interrogative Positive Sentences:-

1. क्या वह सुबह से शाम तक जाता रहेगा?
   Will he have been going from morning to evening?
2. क्या वह दो बजे तक खाती रहेगी?
   Will she have been eating since 2 o' clock?
3. क्या राम रात्रि से पढ़ रहा होगा?
   Will Ram have been reading since night?
4. क्या सीता दोपहर से खेल रही होगी?
   Will Sita have been playing since noon?
5. क्या लड़का सोमवार से दौड़ रहा होगा?
   Will the boy have been running since Monday?
6. क्या लड़की जुलाई से गा रही होगी?
   Will the girl have been singing since July?
7. क्या मैं दो दिन से 4 दिन तक आता रहूँगा?
   Shall I have been coming from 2 days to 4 days?
8. क्या हम दो सप्ताह तक नहाते रहेंगे?
   Shall we have been taking bath till 2 weeks?
9. क्या तुम दो माह से सुनते रहोगे?
   Will you have been hearing for 2 months?
10. क्या वे कल से बजाते रहेगे?
    Will they have been playing on since tomorrow?
11. क्या लड़के दो वर्ष से हंस रहे होंगे?
    Will the boys have been laughing for 2 years?

12. क्या लड़कियाँ दो घण्टे से देख रही होगी?
    Will the girls have been looking for 2 hours?

4. **Interrogative Negative Sentences:-**

1. क्या वह सुबह से शाम तक नहीं जा रहा होगा?
   Will he not been going from morning to evening?
2. क्या वह दो बजे तक नहीं खाती रहेगी?
   Will she not been eating upto 2 o' clock?
3. क्या राम रात्रि से नहीं पढ़ रहा होगा?
   Will Ram not been reading since night?
4. क्या सीता दोपहर से नहीं खेल रही होगी?
   Will Sita not been playing since noon?
5. क्या लड़का सोमवार से नहीं दौड़ रहा होगा?
   Will the boy not been running since Monday?
6. क्या लड़की जुलाई से नहीं गा रही होगी?
   Will the girl not been singing since July?
7. क्या मैं दो दिन से चार दिन तक नहीं आता रहूँगा?
   Shall I not been coming from 2 days to 4 days?
8. क्या हम दो सप्ताह तक नहीं नहाते रहेंगे?
   Shall we not been taking bath for 2 weeks?
9. क्या तुम दो माह से नहीं सुन रहे होंगे?
   Will you not been hearing for 2 months?
10. क्या वे कल से नहीं बजाते रहेंगे?
    Will they not been playing on since tomorrow?
11. क्या लड़के दो वर्ष से नहीं हंस रहे होंगे?
    Will the boys not been laughing for 2 years?
12. क्या लड़कियाँ दो घण्टे से नहीं देख रही होगी?
    Will the girls not been looking for 2 hours?

52th Day

5. **Interrogative Positive Sentences:- {with Question words}**

1. वह सुबह से शाम तक कहां जाता रहेगा?
   Where will he have been going from morning to evening?
2. वह दो बजे तक क्या खाती रहेगी?
   What will she have been eating upto 2 o' clock?
3. राम रात्रि से क्या पढ़ रहा होगा?
   What will Ram have been reading since night?
4. सीता दोपहर से क्यों खेल रही होगी?
   Why will Sita have been playing since noon?
5. लड़का सोमवार से कब दौड़ रहा होगा?
   When will the boy have been running since Monday?
6. लड़की जुलाई से क्या गा रही होगी?
   What will the girl have been singing since July?
7. मैं दो दिन से चार दिन तक कहां आता रहूँगा?
   Where shall I have been coming from 2 days to 4 days?
8. हम दो सप्ताह तक कैसे नहाते रहेंगे?
   How shall we have been taking bath till 2 weeks?
9. तुम दो माह से क्या गाते रहोगे?
   What will you have been singing for 2 months?
10. वे कल से क्या बजाते रहेगे?
    What will they have been playing on since tomorrow?
11. लड़के दो वर्ष से क्यों हंस रहे होंगे?
    Why will the boys have been laughing for 2 years?

12. लड़कियाँ दो घण्टे से क्या देख रही होगी?
What will the girls have been looking for 2 hours?

6. **Interrogative negative sentences:- {with question words}**

1. वह सुबह से शाम तक कहां नहीं जाता रहेगा?
Where will he not have been going from morning to evening?
2. वह दो बजे तक क्या नहीं खाती रहेगी?
What will she have not been eating upto 2 o' clock?
3. राम रात्रि से क्या नहीं पढ़ रहा होगा?
What will Ram not have been reading since night?
4. सीता दोपहर से क्यों नहीं खेल रही होगी?
Why will Sita not have been playing since noon?
5. लड़का सोमवार से कब नहीं दौड़ रहा होगा?
When will the boy not have been running since Monday?
6. लड़की जुलाई से क्या नहीं गा रही होगी?
What will the girl not have been singing since July?
7. मैं दो दिन से चार दिन तक क्यों नहीं आता रहूँगा?
Why shall I not have been coming from 2 days to 4 days?
8. हम दो सप्ताह तक कैसे नहीं नहाते रहेगे?
How shall we not have been taking bath till 2 weeks?
9. तुम दो माह से क्या नहीं सुनते रहे होंगे?
What will you not have been hearing for 2 months?
10. वे कल से क्या नहीं बजाते रहेगे?
What will they not have been playing on since tomorrow?
11. लड़के दो वर्ष से क्यों नहीं हंस रहे होंगे?
Why will the boys not have been laughing for 2 years?
12. लड़कियाँ दो घण्टे से क्या नहीं देख रही होगी?
What will the girls not have been looking for 2 hours?

53th Day

(A)

1.	वह जाता तो है।	He does go.
2.	वह निश्चय ही खाती है।	She does eat.
3.	राम अवश्य पढ़ता है।	Ram does read.
4.	सीता खेलती तो थी।	Sita did play.
5.	लड़का निश्चय ही दौड़ता था।	The boy did run.
6.	मैं अवश्य ही लिखता था।	I did write.
7.	हम नहाते तो हैं।	We do take bath.
8.	तुम निश्चय ही सुनते हो।	You do hear.
9.	वे अवश्य ही बजाते है।	They do play on.
10.	लड़के हंसते तो थे।	The boys did laugh.
11.	लड़कियाँ निश्चय ही देखती थी।	The girls did look.
12.	चिड़िया अवश्य ही उड़ती थी।	The birds did fly.

(B)

1.	वह चतुर है।	He is clever.
2.	वह मूर्ख है।	She is fool.
3.	राम मोटा है।	Ram is fat.
4.	सीता पतली है।	Sita is thin.
5.	लड़का लम्बा है।	The boy is tall.

6. लड़की ठिगनी है।	The girl is short.
7. मैं अच्छा हूँ।	I am good.
8. हम खिलाड़ी है।	We are players.
9. तुम गायक हो।	You are singer.
10. वे युवा है।	They are young.
11. लड़के चोर हैं।	The boys are thieves.
12. लड़कियाँ सुन्दर हैं।	The girls are beautiful.

54th Day

(C)

1.	मकान बड़ा था।	The house was big.
2.	कुत्ता पालतू नहीं था।	The dog was not pet.
3.	क्या राज छोटा था?	Was Raj small?
4.	क्या घोड़ा मोटा नहीं था?	Was the horse not fat?
5.	पत्तियाँ पीली थी।	The leaves were yellow.
6.	प्याले पुराने नहीं थे।	The cups were not old.
7.	क्या चिड़ियां काली थी?	Were the birds black?
8.	क्या लड़के विद्यार्थी नहीं थे?	Were the boys not student?

(D)

1.	हम पागल होंगे।	We shall be mad.
2.	कमरे ठण्डे होंगे।	The rooms will be cold.
3.	घर में खिड़की होगी।	The window will be in the house.
4.	वह चालाक होगा।	He will be cunning.
5.	वह चतुर होगी।	She will be clever.
6.	खिड़की गंदी होगी।	The window will be dirty.
7.	मैं शिक्षक नहीं बनूंगा।	I shall not be a teacher.
8.	क्या हम शिकारी होंगे?	Shall we be hunter?
9.	क्या हम चोर नहीं होंगे?	Shall we not be the thieves?

10. घड़ी नयी नहीं होगी?	The watch will not be new?
11. क्या अमरुद मीठा होगा?	Will the guava be sweet?
12. क्या राजा चोर नहीं होगा?	Will the king not be a thief?

55th Day

(A)

1. राम के पास गाय है।	Ram has a cow.
2. उसके पास पेन नहीं है।	He has no pen.
3. क्या वह घोड़ा रखता है?	Has he a horse?
4. क्या उसके पास बंदूक नहीं है?	Has he not gun?
5. मेरे पास एक कार है।	I have a car.
6. तुम्हारे पास चाकू नहीं है।	You have no knife.
7. क्या हमारे पास गाय है?	Have we a cow?
8. क्या वे जूते नहीं रखते है?	Have they no shoes?
9. उसके पास गाय थी।	He had a cow.
10. तुम पेन नहीं रखते हो।	You had no pen.
11. क्या उनके पास कार थी?	Had they car?
12. क्या उनके पास किताब नहीं थी?	Had they not book?
13. उनके पास एक किताब होगी	He will have a book.
14. घर में खिड़की नहीं होगी।	The house will not have window.
15. क्या मेरे पास गाड़ी होगी?	Shall I have a car?
16. क्या कार पर चालक नहीं होगा?	Will the car not have the driver?

56th Day

(A)

1.	मुझे बदलने होंगे।	I should change.
2.	हमें उससे मिलना चाहिऐ।	We should see him.
3.	हमें प्रार्थना करनी चाहिऐ।	We should pray.
4.	वह मदद नहीं करेगा।	He would not help.
5.	रामू प्रयत्न करेगा।	Ramu would try.
6.	क्या आप किताब देंगे?	Would you give the book?
7.	तुमने कहा की वह आयेगी।	You said that she would come?
8.	वे खेल सकते थे।	They could play.
9.	क्या आप मेरी सहायता कर देंगे?	Would you help me?
10.	मैं झूठ नहीं बोल सकता था।	I could not tell a lie.
11.	मैं तेज दौड़ सकता हूँ।	I can run fast.
12.	वह पकड़ सकता है।	He can catch.
13.	तुम्हारी दीर्घायु हो।	May you live long.
14.	तुम जा सकते हो।	You may go.
15.	तुम पास होने के लिए पढ़ते हो।	You read that you may pass.
16.	वर्षा हो सकती है।	It may rain.
17.	वह नाच सकती है।	She might dance.
18.	राम मुझे बुला सकता है।	Ram might call me.
19.	मुझे लौट आना चाहिए।	I must return.

20. हमें बड़ो की आज्ञा माननी चाहिए।	We must obey our elders.
21. तुम्हें आना पड़ेगा।	You must come.
22. उसे मरना पड़ेगा।	He must die.
23. मुझे पेन की आवश्यकता है।	I need a pen.
24. उसे किताब की जरुरत है।	He needs a book.
25. मुझे घर की जरुरत थी।	I needed the house.
26. हमें किताब की आवश्यकता थी।	We needed the book.
27. मुझे खाने कि जरुरत है।	I need to eat.
28. उसे रोने की आवश्यकता है।	He needs to weep.

57th Day

(A)

1. तुममे खेलने की हिम्मत है।
   You dare to play.
2. उसमें कूदने का साहस है।
   He dare to jump.
3. हममें आने की हिम्मत है।
   We dare to come.
4. हमें सत्य बोलना चाहिए।
   We ought to speak the truth.
5. उसका पढ़ना उचित है।
   He ought to read.
6. मेरा पढ़ना उचित नहीं था।
   I ought not to read.
7. तुम्हें जाना चाहिए था।
   You ought to have gone.
8. हमारा पढ़ना उचित था।
   We ought to have read.
9. हमें नहीं रोका जाना चाहिए था।
   We ought not to have wept.
10. मैं पढ़ा करता था।
    I used to read.
11. तुम खेला करते थे।
    You used to play.

12. वह नहीं जाया करता था।
He used not to go.
13. वह किताब पढ़ता होगा।
He would have read the book.
14. तुमने गाय चराई होगी।
You would have grazed the cow.
15. वह फेल नहीं होता।
He would not have failed.
16. उसे खाना खा लेना चाहिए।
He should have eaten the food.
17. तुम्हे किताब पढ़ लेनी चाहिए।
You should have read the book.
18. मुझे वापिस नहीं आना चाहिए।
I should not have returned.
19. वह किताब दे सकता था।
He could have given the book.
20. तुम कल जा सकते थे।
You could have gone yesterday.
21. मैं काम समाप्त नहीं कर सकता था।
I could not have finished the work.
22. वह ग्वालियर जा सकता था।
He might have gone to Gwalior.
23. तुम अपनी किताब खो सकते थे।
You might have lost your book.
24. तुम नहीं आ सकते थे।
You might not have come.
25. उसे खाना अवश्य खाना चाहिए था।
He must have eaten the food.
26. तुम्हें स्कूल अवश्य जाना चाहिए था।
You must have gone to school.

27. हमें किताब अवश्य पढ़नी चाहिए थी।
    We must have read the book.
28. उसे अवश्य नहीं खेलना चाहिए था।
    We must not have played.

58th Day

(A)

1. उसे दौड़ना पड़ता है।	He has to run.
2. लीला को काम करना है।	Leela has to do the work.
3. मुझे किताब खरीदनी पड़ती है।	I have to buy the book.
4. हमें दौड़ना है।	We have to run.
5. उन्हें पेड़ पर चढ़ना है।	They have to climb on tree.
6. उसे खाना था।	He had to eat.
7. तुमको रोना पढ़ता था।	You had to weep.
8. मुझे स्कूल जाना पढ़ता था।	I had to go to school.
9. उसे नहाना पढ़ता था।	He had to take bath.
10. राम को आना था।	Ram had to come.
11. मां को पकाना था।	The mother had to cook.
12. उसे बड़ों की आज्ञा माननी चाहिए।	He has got to obey his elders.
13. राम को पढ़ना पढ़ेगा।	Ram has got to read.
14. मोहन का नाचना अति आवश्यक है।	Mohan has got to dance.
15. राधा को गाना गाना ही है।	Radha has got to sing a song.
16. मुझे सत्य बोलना चाहिए।	I have got to speak truth.
17. हमें मां बाप की सेवा करनी पड़ेगी।	We have got to serve the parents.
18. तुम्हारा पास होना अति आवश्यक हैं।	You have got to pass.
19. उन्हें खेलना ही है।	They have got to play.
20. लड़कों को दौड़ना ही है।	The boys have got to run.

59th Day

(A)

1. खाना खाओ।	Eat the food.
2. जाओ।	Go.
3. कृपया पत्र लिखो।	Please / Kindly write a letter.
4. दूध मत पियो।	Don't drink the milk.
5. मत हसों।	Don't laugh.
6. कृपया खेल मत खेलो।	Please/kindly don't play the game.
7. यह कैसा सुंदर कपड़ा है।	What a fine cloth it is!
8. वह कितना दुःखी है!	How sad he is today!
9. मौसम कैसा अच्छा है।	How pleasant the weather is.
10. वह लड़की कितनी सुंदर है!	How a beautiful girl is she!
11. अफसोस वह मर गया है!	Alas! He is dead!
12. अह! छुट्टी की घंटी बज गयी है।	Hurrah! The last bell has gone.
13. ईश्वर करे आप पास हो जाये।	May you get through success.
14. ईश्वर इन बच्चों को दीर्घायु करें।	May these children live long.
15. दीर्घायु हो।	May you live long.
16. ईश्वर करे राजा बच जाये।	May God save the king.
17. ईश्वर करे भारतीय गणतंत्र दीर्घायु हो।	May Indian Republic live long.

18. ईश्वर इस पापी को क्षमा करें।	May God pardon this sinner.
19. ईश्वर करे आप अपने उद्देश्य में सफल हों।	May you succeed in your aim.
20. ईश्वर करे हमारी मातृभूमि समृद्धिशाली हो।	May our mother land prosperous.
21. आपकी यात्रा मंगलमय हो।	Wish you a happy journey.
22. आपका स्वास्थ्य अच्छा रहे।	Wish you a good health.
23. आपके माता पिता स्वस्थ रहें।	Wish your parents good health.
24. आप बीमारी से मुक्त रहें।	May you get rid of disease.
25. आपका नाम उज्जवल हो।	Wish your way best.

60th Day

(A)

1. चिड़ियाँ आकाश में उड़ा करती हैं।
   Birds fly in the sky.
2. लड़के सेब पसंद किया करते हैं।
   Boys like apples.
3. कुत्ते रास्ते में सोया करते हैं।
   Dogs sleep in the ways.
4. मोर जंगल में नाचा करते हैं।
   Peacocks dance in the forest.
5. शेर जंगल में दहाड़ा करते हैं।
   Lions roar in the forest.
6. उसने पत्र लिखवाया है।
   He made a letter written.
7. तुमने मेंज पर थालियाँ लगवायी।
   You had the dished laid on the table.
8. हमने काम करवाया है।
   We have the work done.
9. मैंने घोड़े को तेज दौड़ाया।
   I made the horse run fast.
10. उसने मुझे रुला दिया।
    He caused me weep.
11. मंदारी ने बंदर नचाया।
    The juggler made the monkey dance.

12. हमने उसे सुलाया।
We caused him sleep.
13. राम श्याम से खाना खवाता है।
Ram gets Shyam to eat the food
14. वह मुझसे गाना गवाता है।
He gets me to sing a song.
15. वे उससे पत्र नहीं लिखवाते है।
They get him not to write a letter.
16. हरी ने मोहन से पत्र लिखवाया।
Hari got Mohan to write a letter.
17. मैंने तुमसे दूध नही बिकवाया।
I got you not to sell the milk.
18. राधा सीता से कपड़े धुलवायेगी।
Radha will get Sita to wash the clothes.
19. हम उससे रामायण नहीं पढ़वायेंगे।
We shall get him not to read Ramayana.
20. वे हमसे काम नहीं करवायेंगे।
They will get us not to do the work.

61th Day

(A)

1. वह पत्र लिखे।
   He should write a letter.
2. हम पढ़ें।
   We should read.
3. राधा नाचे।
   Radha should dance.
4. वे मरें।
   They should die.
5. गड्ढे पानी से भरें।
   The pits should fill with water.
6. वह पढ़ने लिखने और सीखने के लिए स्कूल जाता है।
   He goes to school to read, write and learn.
7. तुम उठने बैठने और सोने के लिए रोये।
   You wept to rise, sit and sleep.
8. राम कूदने, तैरने और नहाने जायेगा।
   Ram will go to jump, swim and take bath.
9. तुम किताब पढ़ना जानते हो।
   You know how to read the book.
10. राम क्रिकेट खेलना जानता था।
    Ram knew how to play the cricket.
11. वे नाचना जानते हैं।
    They know how to dance.

12. हम तैरना जानते थे।
    We knew how to swim.
13. तुम अब अच्छे पढ़ चुके थे।
    You had better read now.
14. मैं मांगने की बजाय भूखा मरुंगा।
    I would rather starve than beg.
15. तुम उसे जाने दो।
    You let him go.
16. हम तुम्हें पढ़ने दें।
    We let you read.
17. नौकर को जाना था।
    The servant was let go.
18. हमें हंसना था।
    We were let laugh.
19. उसे नहाना था।
    He was let take bath.
20. मैंने आकाश में उड़ती हुई चिड़िया मारी।
    I killed the bird flying in the sky.
21. उसने पानी पीते हुए शेर पकड़ा।
    He caught the lion drinking water.
22. तुमने मंच पर नाचती हुई लड़की देखी।
    You saw a girl dancing on stage.
23. मैंने मरा हुआ शेर देखा।
    I saw a dead lion.
24. राधा टूटा हुआ पेन लायी।
    Radha brought a broken pen.
25. हमनें सोयी हुई लड़की देखी।
    We saw a slept girl.
26. हमने दौड़कर उसकी टांग पकड़ी।
    Having run we caught his leg.

27. राम ने आकर पुल बांधा।

    Having come Ram bound the bridge.

28. उसने पानी पीते पीते गाली दी।

    Having drink water he abused.

29. वह साइकिल चलाते हुए स्कूल गया।

    Having driven cycle he went to school.

62nd Day

(A)

1. Is he at home?	No, he isn't.
2. Do you go?	No, I don't
3. Will he sleep?	No, he won't
4. Shall we run?	No, you won't
5. Will you run?	No, you won't
6. Had the farmer dug?	No, he hadn't
7. Was Ram playing?	No, he wasn't
8. Am I dancing?	No you aren't
9. Can you play?	No, I can't
10. May I sleep?	No, you mayn't

(B)

1. Ram plays by the ball?	Doesn't he?
2. The boys went?	Didn't they?
3. The bird will fly?	Won't it?
4. I can laugh?	Can't it?
5. He does not sing a song?	Does he?
6. They did not jump?	Did they?
7. Sita will not dance?	Will she?
8. We could not run?	Could we?
9. The boys had not skipped?	Had they?
10. The monkeys are climbing?	Are they?

63rd Day

(A)

1. क्या आप दौड़ने की कृपा करेंगे?
   Would you mind running?
2. क्या आप पत्र लिखने की कृपा करेंगे?
   Would you mind writing letter?
3. क्या आप फल बेचने की कृपा करेंगे?
   Would you mind selling fruits?
4. क्या आप रामायण पढ़ने की कृपा करेंगे?
   Would you mind reading Ramayan?
5. वे घर जाने के इच्छुक है।
   They are willing to go to home.
6. हम पानी पीने के लिए इच्छुक हैं।
   We are willing to drink water.
7. सीता घर जाने को इच्छुक हैं।
   Sita is willing to go to home.
8. हरी किताब पढ़ने के लिए इच्छुक नहीं है।
   Hari is not willing to read a book.
9. गाये घास चरने के लिए इच्छुक नहीं थी।
   The cows were not willing to grazing.
10. राम के आने में मुझे कोई आपत्ति नहीं है।
    I don't mind Ram coming.
11. रामू के पढ़ने में हमें कोई आपत्ति नहीं थी।
    We didn’t mind Ramu reading.

12. मनोज के आने में उसे ऐतराज है।
    He minds Manoj coming.
13. दिनेश के रोने में मनोज को ऐतराज था।
    Manoj minded Dinesh weeping.
14. मैं राम के घर जाने में बुरा नहीं मानूंगा।
    I don't mind Ram going to home.
15. मेरे हंसने में वे बुरा नहीं मानेंगे।
    They don't mind my laughing.
16. तुम्हारे नाचने में हम बुरा मानेंगे।
    We mind you dancing.
17. उसके रोने में मैं बुरा मानूंगा।
    I mind his weeping.

64th Day

(A)

1. शक्कर गन्ने से बनी है।

   The sugar is made from sugarcane.

2. घी दूध से बना था।

   The ghee was made from the milk.

3. शर्बत शक्कर से बना होगा।

   The syrup will be made from sugar.

4. चाकू स्टील का बना है।

   The knife is made of steel.

5. प्याले प्लास्टिक के बने हैं।

   The cups are made of plastic.

6. मकान मिट्‌टी का बना था।

   The house was made of sand.

7. संदूक लोहे के बने थे।

   The boxes were made of iron.

8. पेन प्लास्टिक का बना होगा।

   The pen will be made of plastic.

9. चारपाई लकड़ी की बनी होगी।

   The cot will be made of wood.

10. यह एक प्रकार का जानवर है जिसे हम नहीं जानते हैं।

    This is a kind of animal we don't know.

11. यह एक प्रकार का पौधा है जिसे वह नहीं जानती हैं।

    This is a kind of plant she doesn't know.

12. वह एक प्रकार का खेल था जिसे वे नहीं खेल सके।
This was a kind of game they could not play.
13. वह एक प्रकार का बाजा है जिसे मैं नही बजा सकता।
It is a kind of musical instrument I can't play on.
14. इस किस्म के उपन्यास ऐतिहासिक कहलाते हैं।
This type of novel is called an historical.
15. राम उत्तम किस्म के व्यक्ति थे।
Ram was a fine type of person.
16. इस किस्म का दुपट्टा आयात किया जाता है।
This type of cloth/scarf is imported.

65th Day

(A)

1. इतना मीठा था कि उसने संपूर्ण खा लिया।

   It was so sweet that he ate whole of it.

2. निश्चित है कि वह जीवित रहेगी।

   It is certain that she will survive.

3. संभव है कि वह आ सकता है।

   It is possible he may come.

4. निश्चित है कि वह अपराधी था।

   It is certain he was guilty.

5. मुझे पूर्ण विश्वास है कि पानी आज बरसेगा।

   I am quite sure that rain will fall today.

6. मुझे विश्वास है कि राम आयेगा।

   I am sure that Ram will come.

7. मुझे पूर्ण विश्वास है कि हम जीतेंगे।

   I am sure we shall win.

8. मुझे डर है कि वह फेल हो जायेगी।

   I am afraid that she will fail.

9. हमें डर है कि उसका बेटा मर जायेगा।

   We are afraid that her son will die.

10. नाविक भयभीत है कि नाव डूब न जायें।

    The sailor is afraid the boat may not sink.

11. सीता को डर है कि राम शीशा तोड़ देगा।

    Sita is afraid Ram will break the mirror.

12. हमें भय है कि वह कल नहीं आयेगा।

    We are afraid he may not come tomorrow.

66th Day

(A)

1. मैं किताब खरीदने वाला हूँ।
   I am going to buy the book.
2. तुम एक गीत गाने ही वाले हो।
   You are going to sing a song.
3. वह भोजन करने वाला है।
   He is about to eat the food.
4. हम पत्र लिखने वाले हैं।
   We are about to write the letters.
5. राम खेलने वाला था।
   Ras was about to play.
6. वे आने ही वाले थे।
   They were about to come.
7. मैं स्वयं दौड़ता हूँ।
   I myself run.
8. तुम स्वयं लड़ते हो।
   You yourself fight.
9. वे स्वयं नाचे।
   They themselves danced.
10. राम ने स्वयं रावण मारा।
    Ram killed Ravan himself.
11. तुम पत्र स्वयं लिखते हो।
    You write yourself a letter.

12. राधा गाना स्वयं गायेगी।
Radha will sing herself a song.
13. मुझे लिखने दो।
Let me write.
14. उसे गाने दो।
Let him sing.
15. हमें गेंद खेलना चाहिए।
Let us play the ball.
16. आओ चलें।
Let us go.
17. चलो स्कूल चलें।
Let us go to school.
18. मुझे पढ़ने दो।
Let me read.
19. हमें नहाना चाहिए।
Let us take bath.
20. रमेश को हँसने दो।
Let Ramesh laugh.
21. उसे तैरने दो।
Let him swim.
22. यदि वह घर गया होता तो उसने खाना खाया होता।
If he had gone to home he would have eaten the food.
23. यदि तुमने मेहनत की होती तो तुम पास हो गये होते।
If you had worked hard you would have passed.
24. यदि मैंने सांप को पकड़ा होता तो वह मुझे काट लेता।
If I had caught the snake It would have bitten me.
25. यदि ट्रेन रुकी होती तो वह कूद गया होता।
If the train had stopped he would have jumped out of it.

67th Day

(A)

1. मुझे एक पेन और एक पेन्सिल चाहिए।
   I want a pen and a pencil.
2. मेरे पास कागज और कलम भी है।
   I have paper and pen.
3. हमने अपनी किताब खोली और पढ़ने लगे।
   We opened our book and began to read.
4. वह बुद्धिमान और परिश्रमी दोनों ही है।
   He is both intelligent and diligent.
5. रामू चोर और ईमानदार दोनों ही है।
   Ramu is both thief and honest.
6. उसने अपनी किताबें और कापियाँ दोनों ही खो दी।
   He lost both his books and copies.
7. मोहन के साथ साथ राम भी खेलता है।
   Mohan as well as Ram plays.
8. वह अमीर होने के साथ साथ गरीब भी है।
   He is rich as well as poor.
9. तुम खेलने के साथ दौड़ते भी हो।
   You play as well as run.
10. राम केवल चोर ही नहीं अपितु कातिल भी है।
    Ram is not only thief but also murderer.

11. वह केवल शिक्षक ही नहीं अपितु प्राचार्य भी है।
    He is not only teacher but also principal.
12. हम केवल मोटे ही नहीं अपितु पतले भी है।
    We are not only fat but also thin.

68th Day

(A)

1. वह न केवल हंसता है बल्कि रोता भी है।
   He not only laughes but he weeps as well.
2. यह कलम न केवल लिखती है यह प्रकाश भी देती है।
   The pen not only writes it produces light as well.
3. राम पढ़ने के लिए कमजोर भी है।
   Ram is too weak to read.
4. हम दौड़ने के लिए मोटे भी थे।
   We were too fat to run.
5. तुम बोलने के लिए गूंगे भी हो।
   You are too dumb to speak.
6. दिनेश खेलने के लिए बीमार भी था।
   Dinesh was too ill to play.
7. वह निर्धन है परन्तु ईमानदार है।
   He is poor but honest.
8. वह तेज दौड़ा परन्तु बस नहीं पकड़ पाया।
   He run fast but he could not catch the bus.
9. मैं नाराज था तो भी मैं चुप था।
   I was angry still I kept quite.
10. वह बीमार है फिर भी कठिन परिश्रम करता है।
    He is ill still he works hard.

11. रामू गरीब था तब भी उसने फीस दे दी।
Ramu was poor still he paid the fees.
12. राम गरीब है तो भी ईमानदार है।
Ram is poor yet he is honest.
13. हम पास हो गये तो भी रोये।
We passed yet we wept.
14. वह बीमार है तो भी खुश है।
He is ill yet he is happy.

69th Day

(A)

1. मैंने अच्छे से अच्छा प्रयास किया तथापि असफल रहा।
   I did my best nevertheless I failed.
2. उसने साइकिल खरीदी तब भी वह नहीं पहुंच सका।
   He bought the cycle nevertheless he could not reach.
3. कोमल ने कठिन मेहनत की जिसपर भी वह फेल हो गयी।
   Komal worked hard nevertheless she failed.
4. चेतावनी के बावजूद भी वह गया।
   Not with standing warning he went.
5. वह गरीब होने के बावजूद भी ईमानदार है।
   He is poor notwithstanding he is honest..
6. वह पास हो गया जबकि उसने कठिन मेहनत नहीं की थी।
   He passed where as /while he did not work hard.
7. या तो तुम पागल हो या मजाक कर रहे हो।
   Either you are mad or you are cracking a joke.
8. या तो तुम चतुर हो या मैं चतुर हूं।
   Either you or I clever.
9. मैं या तो मोटा या पतला हूँ।
   I am either fat or thin.
10. न तो मैं और न हीं मेरे मित्र घर गये।
    Neither I nor my friend went to home.
11. न तो वह सुंदर है और न ही वह कुरुप है।
    She is neither beautiful nor ugly.

12. राधा या मोहन नाचेंगे।

    Radha or Mohan will dance.

13. अंदर आओ अथवा बाहर जाओ।

    Come in or go out.

14. हम जीतेंगे या मर जायेंगे।

    We shall win or die.

15. वह आयेगा अथवा पत्र भेजेगा।

    He will come or he will send a letter.

70th Day

(A)

1. न तो मैं पढ़ सकता हूँ न उच्चारण कर सकता हूँ।
   I cannot read nor pronounce.
2. न तो मैं जाता हूँ न श्याम जाता है।
   I nor Shyam goes / I go nor Shyam goes.
3. कठिन मेहनत करो नहीं तो फेल हो जाओगे।
   Work hard else you will fail.
4. तेज चलो नहीं तो तुम्हे देर हो जायेगी।
   Run fast else you will be late.
5. घंटी बजाओ अन्यथा कोई फाटक नहीं खोलेगा।
   Ring the bell otherwise nobody will open the gate.
6. यदि इस लड़के ने मुझे बचाया न होता तो मैं डूब जाता।
   This boy saved me otherwise I would have been drowned.
7. वह बीमार है अतः वह नहीं आ सकता है।
   He is ill therefore he cannot come.
8. मैं जिद्दी था अतः मुझे सजा मिली।
   I was obstinate therefore I was punished.
9. हम थक गये थे इस कारण हम नहीं आये।
   We were tired so we did not come.
10. वह तेज दौड़ा इस कारण वह गिरा।
    He ran fast so he fell.
11. वह चालाक है अतएव उसे कोई पसंद नहीं करता।
    He is very cunning so nobody likes him.

12. उसे कोई डर नहीं लगा क्योंकि वह वीर था।
He fell no fear for he was a brave.
13. तुम पास नही हो सकते क्योंकि तुमने मेहनत नहीं की।
You can not pass for you did not work hard.
14. वह आयेगा अथवा पत्र भेजेगा।
He will come or he will send a letter.

71th Day

(A)

1. जब तक राम जाता है तब तक मैं आता हूँ।

   As long as Ram goes I come.

2. जब तक हम आये तब तक वे गये।

   As long as we came they went.

3. जब तक वह आयेगा तब तक मैं गाऊँगा।

   As long as he comes I shall sing.

4. उन्होंने प्रतीक्षा की जब तक वह नहीं आया।

   They wait until he come.

5. मैं प्रतीक्षा करुंगा जब तक तुम नहीं आओगे।

   I shall wait until you come.

6. जैसे ही तुम जाते हो वैसे ही वह आता हैं।

   As soon as you go he comes.

7. ज्यों ही वे गये त्यों ही हम आये।

   As soon as they went we came.

8. ज्यों ही वह आयेगा त्यों ही हम जायेंगे।

   As soon as he comes we shall go.

9. त्यों ही जाता हूँ त्यों ही वह आता है।

   No sooner do I go than he comes.

10. जैसे ही वे आये वैसे ही मैं गया।

    No sooner did they come than I went.

11. मैं जाता हूँ जब तक तुम यहीं ठहरो।

    I go till you stay here.

12. उसने मेरा इंतजार किया जब तक मैं आया।

    He waited me till I come.

13. तुम प्रतीक्षा करोगे जब तक मैं आऊंगा।

    You will wait till I come.

72nd Day

(A)

1. चूंकि मैं खाना खाता हूँ इसलिए मैं बात नहीं करता हूँ।
   Since I eat the food I do not talk.
2. चूंकि विक्रम रोया इसलिये मैंने नहीं पीटा।
   Since Vikram wept I did not beat.
3. दरवाजा मत खोलो ताकि टूट न जाये ।
   Don't open the door lest it should break.
4. बाहर मत जाओ ताकि सर्दी न लग जाये।
   Don't go out lest you catch cold.
5. कठिन मेहनत करो ताकि तुम पास हो सको।
   Work hard so that you may pass.
6. तेज दौड़ो ताकि वह पकड़ न सके।
   Run fast so that he might not catch.
7. पत्र लिखो ताकि तुम समाचार पा सको।
   Write a letter so that you may get news.
8. मैं काम नहीं कर सकता क्यांकि मैं बीमार हूँ।
   I can not do the work because I am ill.
9. रामू पकड़ा गया क्योंकि वह चोर था।
   Ramu was caught because he was thief.
10. हम जैसे ही पहुंचे द्वार खुल गया।
    As we reached the door opened.
11. वह इतना गरीब है कि वह साइकिल नहीं खरीद सकता है
    He is so poor that he can not buy a cycle.

12. रामू इतनी तेज दौड़ा कि वह इनाम जीत सके।
    Ramu ran so fast that he could win the prize.
13. तुम ऐसे ही आदमी थे कि तुम आ नहीं सके।
    You were such a man that you could not come.
14. वह इसी प्रकार का कमजोर है कि वह दौड़ नहीं सकता हैं।
    He is such weak that he can not run.
15. वह आयेगा अथवा पत्र भेजेगा।
    He will come or he will send a letter.

73rd Day

(A)

1. यदि वह जाता है तो मैं जाता हूँ।
   If he goes I go.
2. यदि हम आये तो वे गये।
   If we come they went.
3. यदि वह आयेगा तो हम जायेंगे।
   If he comes we shall go.
4. यदि वह नहीं जाता है तो मैं नहीं जाता हूँ।
   Unless he goes I don't go.
5. यदि वे नहीं गये तो हम नहीं आये।
   Unless they went we did not come.
6. यदि तुम नहीं आओगे तो हम नहीं जायेंगे।
   Unless you come we shall not go.
7. मैं आऊंगा चाहे वह आयेगा या न आयेगा।
   I shall come whether he comes or not.
8. जहां तक मुझे याद है कल वर्षा हुई थी।
   As far as I remember it rained yesterday.
9. जहां तक मैं जानता हूँ समाचार गलत हैं।
   As far as I know the news is wrong.
10. जहां तक इससे सम्बंध है कि मैं असहाय हूँ।
    So far as this is concerned I am helpless.

11. जहां तक उसे पता था कि परीक्षा कल शुरु होगी।
    So far as he knew the exam will start tomorrow.
12. पंकज से कम महत्वपूर्ण किसी ने गाना नहीं गाया।
    No less a person than Pankaj sing a song.
13. मुझसे कम महत्वपूर्ण खिलाड़ी ने खेल नहीं खेला।
    No less the player than I played the game.

74th Day

(A)

1. वह उतना बड़ा है जितना मैं बड़ा हूँ।
   He is as old as I (I am).
2. वह उतना चतुर है जितना वह ईमानदार है।
   He is as clever as he is honest.
3. तुम उतने लम्बे नहीं हो जितना वे कहते हैं।
   You are not so tall as they say.
4. जैसा तुम करोगे वैसा तुम पाओगे।
   As you do so you will get.
5. वह जितना हो सका उतना अपने भाई बहिन को चाहता है।
   He likes his sister as much as he likes his brother.
6. यद्यपि वह गरीब है फिर भी वह संतोषी है।
   Though he is poor he is contented.
7. यद्यपि मैंने उसको गाली दी फिर भी उसने मुझे प्यार किया ।
   Though I abused him he loved me.
8. यद्यपि वह गरीब है किन्तु फिर भी वह ईमानदार है।
   Although he is poor he is honest / Although he is poor yet he is honest.
9. यह वही लड़की है जो प्रथम आयी थी।
   This is same girl as she came first.
10. यह वही किताब है जो तुमने खरीदी।
    This is same book as you bought.

11. तुम पास हो गये ठीक मैं ऐसी आशा नहीं करता था।
    You passed well I did not hope so.
12. तुमने चोरी की ठीक मैं यह नहीं जानता था।
    You stole well I did not know this.
13. आप जहां जाना चाहो जाओ केवल यहां मत ठहरो।
    Go where you like only don't stay here.
14. बातें करो केवल चिल्लाओ मत।
    Talk only don't cry.

75th Day

(A)

1. वह कुछ तेज ही चलाता है।
   He drives rather fast.
2. वह कुछ कुरूप ही है।
   She is rather ugly.
3. हम अधिक पागल ही थे।
   We were rather mad.
4. तुम निश्चय ही चतुर हो।
   You are rather clever.
5. वे वस्तुतः बुद्धिमान है।
   They are rather wise.
6. राधा कुरूप तो है ही नहीं उल्टे सुंदर है।
   Radha is not ugly rather beautiful.
7. हमारे बदले हमारा भाई काम करता है।
   Our brother does the work rather we.
8. मोहन के बजाय सोहन नाचता है।
   Sohan dance rather Mohan.
9. वह मोटा तो है पर पतला नहीं।
   He is fat rather than thin.
10. वे धनी तो है पर चोर नहीं।
    They are rich rather than thieves.
11. राधा नाचती तो है पर गाती नहीं।
    Radha dances rather than sings.

12. मैं अभी स्कूल गया ही था कि मोहन आ गया।
I had hardly gone to school then Mohan came.
13. हम मुश्किल से घर पहुंचे ही थे कि वर्षा शुरु हो गयी।
We have hardly reached home when it began to rain.
14. अभी हम पहुंचे ही थे कि गाड़ी छूट गयी।
We had hardly reached when the train left.
15. मुश्किल से मैं आया ही था कि वह मर गया।
I had hardly come when he died.

76th Day

(A)

1. मैं थका हूँ तो भी मैं जाऊंगा।

   I am tired all the same I shall go.

2. राम बीमार था इसके बावजूद भी वह यहां आया।

   Ram was ill all the same he came here.

3. वह बिलकुल भी नहीं दौड़ा।

   He not at all ran.

4. तुमने कतई काम नहीं किया।

   You not at all did the work.

5. उसने कठिन मेहनत की इसके बावजूद भी वह फेल हो गया।

   He worked hard in spite of he failed.

6. वह तेज दौड़ा अंत में जीता।

   He ran fast at last he won.

7. उसने कठिन मेहनत की अंत में वह पास हुआ।

   He worked hard at last he passed.

8. साधारणतया वह एक अच्छा लड़का है।

   Generally he is a good boy.

9. राम ने चोरी नहीं की साधारणतया वह धनी था।

   Ram did not steal generally he was rich.

10. मैंने संक्षेप मे उसे कहानी सुनायी।

    In short I told him the story/I told him the story in short.

11. उसने मेहनत की परिणाम स्वरुप वह फेल हो गया।
    He worked hard consequently he failed.
12. उसने बिलकुल भी खाना नहीं खाया।
    Not at least he ate the food.
13. मैं तेज दौड़ा परिणामतः मैं चोर नहीं पकड़ पाया।
    I rain fast consequently I could not catch the thief.

77th Day

(A)

1. वह पूर्णतया चोर है।
   Thoroughly he is thief / He is thoroughly thief.
2. राम बाहर आया कि वह पूर्णतया भीग गया।
   Ram came out thoroughly he became wet.
3. हमने परिश्रम किया अंत में हम फेल हो गये।
   We worked hard eventually we failed.
4. वे तेज दौड़े अंत में वे सफल हो गये।
   They ran fast eventually they succeed.
5. वह वास्तव में चोर था।
   In fact he was thief.
6. वह पास हो गया वास्तव में मैं नहीं सोचता था।
   He passed in fact I did not think.
7. मैं लगभग स्टेशन पहुंच चुका था।
   I had almost reached the station.
8. तुम लगभग आ चुके थे।
   You had almost come.
9. मैं घर पहुंचा तब वह लगभग पढ़ चुका था।
   I reached the home almost he had read.
10. वह नहीं पढ़ा इसके अतिरिक्त वह पास हो गया।
    He did not read further more he passed.

11. वह तेज नहीं दौड़े इसके अतिरिक्त वह जीता।

    He did not run fast further more he won.

12. चाहे जो भी हो मैं आऊंगा।

    At any cost I shall come.

13. वास्तव में मैं कल जाऊंगा।

    Truely I shall go tomorrow.

78th Day

(A)

1. वह ऐसा होने पर भी नहीं सुधरा।

   He was not improved in the event of / In the event of he was not improved.

2. घायल होने पर भी वह नहीं समझा।

   He was not knew in the event of wounded.

3. वह निश्चय ही चोर है।

   Indeed he is a thief.

4. वह सचमुच सुंदर है परन्तु उसे घमण्ड नहीं है।

   She is beautiful indeed but she is not proud.

5. तुम निश्चय ही मोटे हो पर तुम पागल हो।

   You are fat indeed but you are fool.

6. तुम्हारे कठिन मेहनत करने पर ही मैं मदद करुंगा।

   In case you worked hard I shall help.

7. उसके स्टेशन पहुंचने के बावजूद भी वह समय पर नहीं पहुंचा।

   In case he reached the station he could not reach in time.

8. मैं तुम्हे किताब दूंगा पर यह शर्त है कि तुम कल वापिस करो।

   I shall give you book provided you return tomorrow.

9. वह तुम्हे धन देगी पर यह शर्त है कि तुम उसे आश्वासन दो।

   She will give you money provided you assure her.

10. भौंकने वाले कुत्ते कभी नहीं काटते हैं।

    Barking dogs seldom bite.

11. गरजने वाले बादल कभी नहीं बरसते हैं।

    Roaring clouds seldom rain.

79th Day

(A)

1. वह सदैव झूठ बोलता है।
   He always speaks a lie.
2. हम हमेशा सोते हैं।
   We always sleep.
3. वे सदैव चिल्लाते रहते हैं।
   They always cry.
4. तुम हमेशा चाय पीते थे।
   You always took tea.
5. वह अक्सर चोरी करता है।
   He frequently steals.
6. मैं अक्सर तुम्हें मिलता हूँ।
   I frequently meet you.
7. वे अक्सर किताब पढ़ते हैं।
   They frequently read the book.
8. मेरे दादाजी अक्सर रामायण पढ़ते थे।
   My grandfather frequently read Ramayan.
9. मैं अक्सर जाता रहता हूँ।
   I often go.
10. वे अक्सर सोते रहते हैं।
    They often sleep.
11. तुम अक्सर हंसते रहते हो।
    You often laugh.

80th Day

(A)

1. मैं आऊंगा भले ही वह न आये।
   I shall come even if he did not come.
2. चाहे वह जाये या न जाये मैं जाऊंगा।
   Even if he does not go I shall go.
3. जैसे ही वह आया मैं चला गया।
   Even as he comes I went.
4. मैं आया उसी दम वह चला गया।
   I came even as he went.
5. राम चोर है यद्यपि वह धनी है।
   Ram is thief eventhough he is rich.
6. य़द्यपि वह मोटा है तो भी वह तेज दौड़ता है।
   Even though he is fat he runs fast.
7. सरदार सिंह नाराज था तो भी वह आया।
   Sardar Singh was angry even so he came.
8. वीरेन्द्र तभी रोया जब उसने पीटा।
   Even so Virendra wept he beat.
9. हम धनी थे तो भी हमने चोरी की।
   We were rich even then we stole.
10. वे बीमार थे तो भी वे आये।
    They were ill even then they came.

11. वह देखती है मानो उसे संदेह था।
    She looks as if she suspected.
12. वह रोयी मानो उसे भय था।
    She wept as if she was afraid.
13. सीता देखती है जैसे कि वह जानती थी।
    Sita looks as though she knew.
14. यहां से जाओ कहीं और मांगो।
    Go from here else where beg.
15. यहां मत चिल्लाओ अन्यत्र चिल्लाओ।
    Don't cry here elsewhere cry.

81th Day

1 (Prefix) (उपसर्ग)

1. Fore + Head = Forehead
2. Pre + judice = Prejudice
3. Up + hold = Uphold
4. Re + main = Remain
5. Non + sense = Nonsense
6. Inter + cast = Intercast
7. Em + brace = Embrace
8. En + gage = Engage
9. Un + able = Unable
10. Im + Possible = Impossible
11. Miss + guide = Misguide
12. Diss + count = Discount

Suffix (प्रत्यय)

1. Favour + able = Favourable
2. Man + age = Manage
3. Perform + ance = Performance
4. Child + hood = Childhood
5. King + dom = Kingdom
6. Manage + ment = Management
7. Fore + ward = Forward
8. Creat + tion = Creation
9. Member + ship = Membership

10. Great + ness	=	Greatness
11. Use + ful	=	Useful
12. Kind + ly	=	Kindly
13. Air + y	=	Airy
14. Paise + sion	=	Passion

82nd days

(Verbs)

	1st Form (Present)	*Meaning*	*II Form (Past)*	*III Form Past (Participle)*
1.	Abuse	गाली देना	Abused	Abused
2.	Arise	निकलना	Arose	Arisen
3.	Abide	बसना	Abode	Abode
4.	Annoy	नाराज होना	Annoyed	Annoyed
5.	Alike	पसंद करना	Aliked	Aliked
6.	Arrive	आ पंहुचना	Arrived	Arrived
7.	Alive	रहना	Alived	Alived
8.	Aside	अलग होना	Asided	Asided
9.	Adorn	सजाना	Adorned	Adorned
10.	Abhor	घृणा करना	Abhored	Abhored
11.	Appeal	अपील करना	Appealed	Appealed
12.	Add	जोड़ना	Added	Added
13.	Beach	विरले लगना	Beached	Beached
14.	Bear	सहना	Bare	Bare
15.	Bear	ले जाना	Bare	Bare
16.	Beg	मांगना	Begged	Begged
17.	Behave	बर्ताव करना	Behaved	Behaved
18.	Believe	विश्वास करना	Believed	Believed
19.	Burry	दफनाना	Burried	Burried

	1st Form (Present)	*Meaning*	*II Form (Past)*	*III Form (Participle)*
20.	Build	बनाना	Built	Built
21.	Bear	जन्म लेना	Bare	Born
22.	Ban	रोकना	Banned	Banned
23.	Cut	काटना	Cut	Cut
24.	Carry	ले जाना	Carried	Carried
25.	Come	आना	Came	Come
26.	Climb	चढ़ना	Climbed	Climbed
27.	Count	गिनना	Counted	Counted
28.	Close	बन्द करना	Closed	Closed
29.	Catch	पकड़ना	Caught	Caught
30.	Cry	चिल्लाना	Cried	Cried
31.	Crush	कुचलना	Crushed	Crushed
32.	Curse	अभिशाप देना	Cursed	Cursed
33.	Clap	ताली बजाना	Clapped	Clapped
34.	Dig	खोदना	Dug	Dug
35.	Drive	चलाना	Drove	Driven
36.	Drink	पीना	Drank	Drunk
37.	Deny	ड्रामा करना	Dennied	Dennied
38.	Design	सजाना	Designed	Designed
39.	Decorate	लगाना	Decorated	Decorated
40.	Do	करना	Did	Done
41.	Damage	नष्ट करना	Damaged	Damaged
42.	Dye	रंगना	Dyed	Dyed
43.	Die	मरना	Died	Died
44.	Enter	प्रवेश करना	Entered	Entered
45.	Employ	रोजगार	Employed	Employed
46.	Fail	फेल होना	Failed	Failed
47.	Faint	मुर्छित होना	Fainted	Fainted

	1st Form (Present)	*Meaning*	*II Form (Past)*	*III Form (Participle)*
48.	Fade	मुरझाना	Faded	Faded
49.	Fly	उड़ना	Flew	Flown
50.	Fry	तलना	Fried	Fried
51.	Flop	लपेटना	Flopped	Flopped
52.	Burn	जलाना	Burned	Burned
53.	Go	जाना	Went	Gone
54.	Give	देना	Gave	Given
55.	Glow	दहकना	Glew	Glown
56.	Gain	लाभ	Gained	Gained
57.	Get	पाना	Got	Gotten/ got
58.	Graze	चरना	Grazed	Grazed
59.	Guess	अनुमान लगाना	Guessed	Guessed
60.	Glass	चमकना	Glassed	Glassed
61.	Grant	अनुदान	Granted	Granted
62.	Horse	घुड़सवारी	Horsed	Horsed
63.	Horn	आवाज देना	Horned	Horned
64.	Hit	मारना	Hit	Hit
65.	Humble	विनीत होना	Humbled	Humbled
66.	Hot	गर्माना	Hotted	Hotted
67.	Imagine	कल्पना करना	Imagined	Imagined
68.	Illusion	भ्रमित होना	Illusioned	Illusioned
69.	Idol	मूर्ति पूजा करना	Idoled	Idoled
70.	Joke	मजाक करना	Joked	Joked
71.	Job	काम लगना	Jobbed	Jobbed
72.	Join	मिलना	Joined	Joined
73.	Kick	लात मारना	Kicked	Kicked
74.	Kind	दयालू होना	Kinded	Kinded
75.	Kiss	चूमना	Kissed	Kissed

	1st Form (Present)	*Meaning*	*II Form (Past)*	*III Form (Participle)*
76.	Live	रहना	Lived	Lived
77.	Love	प्यार करना	Loved	Loved
78.	Lose	खोना	Lost	Lost
79.	Loss	क्षति होना	Lossed	Lossed
80.	Like	पसंद करना	Liked	Liked
81.	Leave	छोड़ना	Left	Left
82.	Let	देना	Let	Let
83.	Lunch	दोपहर का भोजन	Lunched	Lunched
84.	Line	रेखा खींचना	Lined	Lined
85.	Light	प्रकाशित करना	Lighted	Lighted
86.	Lead	नेतृत्व करना	Leaded	Leaded
87.	Manage	व्यवस्था करना	Managed	Managed
88.	Miss	चूकना	Missed	Missed
89.	Make	बनाना	Made	Made
90.	Mount	चढ़ना	Mounted	Mounted
91.	Move	चलना	Moved	Moved
92.	Knit	बुनना	Knit	Knit
93.	Know	जानना	Knew	Known
94.	Num	सेव करना	Nummed	Nummed
95.	Open	खोलना	Opened	Opened
96.	Pluck	तोड़ना	Plucked	Plucked
97.	Push	धक्का मारना	Pushed	Pushed
98.	Pull	खींचना	Pulled	Pulled
99.	Peep	झलक	Peeped	Peeped
100.	Quench	प्यास बुझाना	Quenched	Quenched
101.	Quick	जल्दी करना	Quicked	Quicked
102.	Reach	पहुंचना	Reached	Reached
103.	Roar	दहाड़ना	Roared	Roared

	1st Form (Present)	*Meaning*	*II Form (Past)*	*III Form (Participle)*
104.	Write	लिखना	Wrote	Written
105.	Read	पढ़ना	Read	Read
106.	Remove	हटाना	Removed	Removed
107.	Remember	याद करना	Remembered	Remembered
108.	Sink	डूबना	Sank	Sunk
109.	See	देखना	Saw	Seen
110.	Sow	बोना	Sew	Sewn
111.	Search	तलाशना	Searched	Searched
112.	Slaught	हत्या करना	Slaughted	Slaughted
113.	Tear	आंसू बहाना	Tore	Torn
114.	Tie	बांधना	Tied	Tied
115.	Urge	प्रार्थना करना	Urged	Urged
116.	Voice	आवाज करना	Voiced	Voiced
117.	Wear	पहनना	Wore	Worn
118.	Yoke	जोड़ना	Yoked	Yoked
119.	Zeal	उत्साहित होना	Zealed	Zealed

83rd days

(Homonyms — समोच्चारित शब्द)

	Words	*Meaning*	*Words*	*Meaning*
1.	Access	पहुंच	Excess	अधिकता
2.	Adopt	ग्रहण करना	Adapt	अनुकूल करना
3.	Advice	सलाह	Advise	सलाह देना
4.	Air	हवा	Heir	उत्तराधिकारी
5.	Affect	प्रभाव डालना	Effect	प्रभाव
6.	Altar	वलिवेदी	Alter	बदलना
7.	Bail	जमानत	Bale	सामान का गट्ठा
8.	Bare	नंगा	Bear	रोक
9.	Birth	जन्म	Berth	सोने का स्थान
10.	Born	पैदा हुआ	Borne	धारित
11.	Break	तोड़ना	Brake	रोकने का यंत्र
12.	Bridal	दुल्हन संबंधी	Bridle	लगाम
13.	Cast	देना	Caste	जाति
14.	Canvas	मोटा कपड़ा	Canvass	प्रचार करना
15.	Check	जांच	Cheque	रुक्का
16.	Cattle	पशु	Kettle	केतली
17.	Cite	प्रमाण पत्र	Sight	दृष्टि
18.	Cloth	कपड़ा	Clothe	पोशाक
19.	Corpse	शव	Corps	पलटन

	Words	Meaning	Words	Meaning
20.	Council	परिषद	Counsel	सलाह
21.	Dairy	दुग्धालय	Diary	दैनन्दिनी
22.	Dear	प्रिय	Deer	हिरण
23.	Decent	सम्माननीय	Descent	कुलीनता
24.	Difference	भिन्नता	Deference	आदर
25.	Die	मरना	Dye	रंगना
26.	Eminent	श्वेत	Imminent	करीब
27.	Eligible	उपयुक्त	Illigible	अस्पष्ट
28.	Fair	ठीक मिला	Fare	किराया
29.	Floor	फर्श	Flour	आटा
30.	Gaol	बंदीगृह	Goal	लक्ष्य
31.	Gate	फाटक	Gait	चाल
32.	Hail	ओले	Hale	स्वास्थ्य
33.	Hair	बाल	Hare	खरगोश
34.	Heal	घाव भरना	Heel	एड़ी
35.	Hoard	इकट्ठा करना	Horde	झुण्ड
36.	Human	मानवीय	Humane	दयालु
37.	Idle	आलसी	Idol	प्रतिमा
38.	Knotty	कठिन	Naughty	नटखट
39.	Lesson	पाठ	Lessen	कम करना
40.	Loose	ढीला	Lose	खोना
41.	Liar	झूठा	Lawyer	वकील
42.	Later	बाद	Letter	पत्र
43.	Main	मुख्य	Mane	गर्दन पर बाल
44.	Male	पुरुष	Mail	कवच/डाक
45.	Marry	शादी करना	Merry	आनन्द लेना
46.	Miner	खदान में काम करना	Minor	मामूली
47.	Pail	बाल्टी	Pole	खंभा
48.	Plain	मैंदान, समतल	Plane	हवाई जहाज
49.	Palm	हथेली	Pan	कंड़ाही

	Words	*Meaning*	*Words*	*Meaning*
50	Pole	खम्भा	Poll	सदस्य चुनने का स्थान
51.	Pray	प्रार्थना	Prey	शिकार करना
52.	Principal	प्राचार्य	Principle	सिद्धांत
53.	Pour	उड़ेलना	Pore	रोमछिद्र
54.	Quite	बिल्कुल	Quiet	शांत
55.	Rain	वर्षा	Reign	राज्य करना
56.	Root	जड़	Roat	उपद्रव
57.	Soar	ऊँचा उड़ना	Sore	तट
58.	Soul	आत्मा	Sole	अकेला
59.	Sale	विक्रय	Sail	खेवन
60.	Stationery	लिखने का समान	Stationary	स्थिर
61.	Story	कहानी	Storey	मंजिल
62.	Stair	सीढ़ी	Stare	घूरना
63.	Straight	समुचित मार्ग	Straight	सीधा
64.	Temper	प्रकृति	Tamper	दूषित करना
65.	Team	बहुतायत में उत्पन्न	Team	टीम
66.	Veil	परदा/घूघंट	Vail	विलाप करना
67.	Vain	घमण्डी	Vein	शिरा
68.	Vane	दिशामापन यंत्र	Van	गाड़ी
69.	Vacation	अवकाश	Vocation	व्यवसाय
70.	Wave	लहर	Waive	छोड़ना
71.	Waiste	कमर	Waste	नष्ट करना
72.	Weather	मौसम	Whether	यदि
73.	Wander	घूमना	Wonder	आश्चर्य
74.	Wear	पहनना	Ware	विकय सामग्री
75.	Week	सप्ताह	Weak	कमजोर
76.	Yoke	जुआ	Yolk	अंडे का पीला भाग
77.	Yearn	उदास होना	Yarn	धागा
78.	Date	खजूर	Date	दिनांक
79.	Bear	भालू	Bear	जन्म लेना
80.	Sentence	वाक्य	Sentence	सजा

84th days

(Synonyms — पर्यायवाची शब्द)

	Words	*Meaning*	*Synonyms*
1.	Anger	क्रोध	Indignent, Vexation, Annoyance, Wrath
2.	Effect	प्रभाव	Accomplish, Execute, Achieve
3.	Adversity	दुख	Calamity, Misery, Tribulation
4.	Stingy	लालची	Ararious, Misery, Penurious
5.	Tyrant	निर्दयी	Autocrat, Despot, Monarch
6.	Build	निर्माण	Etreat, Construct
7.	Courage	साहस	Bravery, Gallantry, Fortitude
8.	Bias	ईर्ष्या	Prejudice, Prepossession
9.	Brief	संक्षेप	Concise, Terse, Pithy
10.	Understand	समझना	Comprehend, Apprehend
11.	Restraint	नियंत्रण	Compulsion, Constraint
12.	Customary	प्रचलित	Fashionable, Conventional
13.	Civil	विनम्र	Courteous, Affable, Polite, Humble
14.	Pair	जोड़ा	Couple
15.	Contrary	विपरीत	Opposite, Reverse
16.	Vice	अपराध	Sin, Crime
17.	Rival	प्रतियोगी	Competitor
18.	Confuse	भ्रम	Confound, Derange
19.	Aware	ज्ञान	Conscious
20.	Respect	सत्कार	Deference, Reverence, Veneration

	Words	Meaning	Synonyms
21.	Dangerous	भयानक	Perilous, Hazardous
22.	Skill	होशियारी	Dexterity, Address, Expertness, Cleverness
23.	Hate	घृणा	Despise, Contemn, Seom, Disdain, Abhor
24.	Envy	ईर्ष्या	Jealousy
25.	Error	गलती	Mistakes, Blunder
26.	Frank	दयालु	Candid, Ingenuous
27.	Figure	आकृति	Emblem, Type, Symbol
28.	Faith	विश्वास	Belief, Credulity
29.	Frailty	कमजोरी	Foible, Feebleness, Weakness, Failing
30.	Force	बल	Compel, Coerce, Oblige, Constrain
31.	Mild	मृदु	Kind, Tender, Gentle
32.	Guard	रक्षक	Protect, Save, Secure
33.	Hasty	जल्दीबाजी	Premature, quick, rapid, fast
34.	Fancy	कल्पना	Imagination
35.	Implacable	निर्दयता	Unrelenting, Inexorable
36.	Inevitable	अनिवार्य	Unavoidable
37.	Impossible	असंभव	Impracticable
38.	Increase	वृद्धि करना	Enlarge, Augment
39.	Funny	मजाकिया	Jocose, Ludicrous, Absurd, Rediculous
40.	Stay	घूमना ढ़कना	Winger, Loiter
41.	Illegal	गैर कानूनी	Lawless, Unlawful
42.	Mad	पागल	Insane, Imbecile
43.	Shy	लज्जावान	Modest, Diffident, Bashful, Demurs, Reserved
44.	Event	घटना	Occurence, Circumstance
45.	Clear	स्पष्ट	Evident, Obvious
46.	Chance	अवसर	Opportunity, Occasion, Juncture

	Words	*Meaning*	*Synonyms*
47.	Power	शक्ति	Strength, Force, Authority
48.	Pain	दर्द	Grief, Sorrow, Agony, anguish
49.	Pardon	क्षमा करना	Forgive, Excuse, Appologise
50.	Vertical	लम्बवत्	Perpendicular
51.	Provoke	भड़काना	Prompt, Incite, Instigate
52.	Procedure	कार्यवाही	Proceeding
53.	Solitude	एकांत	Privacy, Retirement, Loneliness, Desolation
54.	Person	प्राणी	Creature, Being, Individual
55.	Rude	निर्लज्ज	Impertinent, Insolent, Impudent
56.	Recover	पुनः प्राप्ति	Regain, Retirement
57.	Rise	चढ़ना	Ascent, Soar, Mount
58.	Regret	पश्चाताप	Lament, Deplore
59.	Respect	आदर	Esteem
60.	Dumb	गूंगा	Reticene, Reserve
61.	Remnant	शेष	Rest, Resident, Remainder, Remain
62.	Revenge	बदला	Avenge, Vengeance
63.	Remember	याद करना	Learn, Recollect
64.	Reproof	तिरस्कार	Reprimand, Censure, Remonstrance
65.	Return	वापिस	Restore, Surrender
66.	See	देखना	Look, Behold, Discarn, Perceive, Aspect
67.	Needless	अनावश्यक	Superflous, Unneccessary
68.	Say	कहना	Tell, Relate, Recount, Describe, Express
69.	Secret	रहस्यपूर्ण	Hidden, Covered, Tacit, Mysterious
70.	Sly	धोखेबाज	Cunning, Crafty, Deceitful
71.	Size	विस्तार	Bulk, Volume

	Words	Meaning	Synonyms
72.	Sanatary	आरोग्यकर	Sanitary, Sanative, Salutory, Salubrious
73.	Slanders	बदनामी	Calumny, Detraction, Defamation,
74.	Severe	कठोर	Harsh, Rigorous, Stern, Austere, Strict
75.	Part	अंश	Bit, Piece, Fragment ,Saperate
76.	Timidity	तुच्छता	Shyness, Bashfulness, Diffidence
77.	Teach	पढ़ाना	Instruct, Inform, Educate
78.	Truth	सच्चाई	Varacity
79.	Useful	उपयोगी	Advantageous, Expedient
80.	Unnatural	अप्राकृतिक	Supernatural, Nonnatural, Preternatural
81.	Variety	विविधता	Variance, Variation
82.	Wisdom	ज्ञान	Learning, Acquitance, Knowledge
83.	Wonder	आश्चर्य	Strange, Surprise, Amuzement, Astonishment

85th days

(Antonyms — विलोम शब्द)

Sl. No.	*Word*	*Meaning*	*Antonyms*
1.	Active	सक्रिय	Passive
2.	Adversity	विपत्ति	Prosperity
3.	Affirm	दृढ़	Decay/Deny
4.	Ascend	चढ़ना	Descend
5.	Attack	आक्रमण	Defend
6.	Admit	स्वीकारना	Refuse
7.	Aware	परिचित	Unaware
8.	Ancient	प्राचीन	Modern
9.	Bold	साहसी	Timid
10.	Bright	चमकीला	Dull
11.	Broad	चौड़ा	Narrow
12.	Base	नीच	noble
13.	Beautiful	सुंदर	Ugly
14.	Beginning	प्रारंभ	End
15.	Blunt	सुथरा	Sharp
16.	Blame	दोष	Praise
17.	Cheerful	प्रसन्नता	Gloomy
18.	Confess	कबूलना	Deny
19.	Certain	निश्चित	Uncertain
20.	Cheap	सस्ता	Dear

Sl. No.	*Word*	*Meaning*	*Antonyms*
21.	Clever	चतुर	Stupid
22.	Clean	साफ	Dirty
23.	Coarse	घटिया	Fine
24.	Common	साधारण	Rare
25.	Conceal	छिपाना	Reveal
26.	Casual	आकस्मिक	Regular
27.	Conquer	जीतना	Surrender
28.	Cruel	निष्ठुर	Kind
29.	Conclude	निष्कर्ष	Begin
30.	Confidence	विश्वास	Diffidence
31.	Continue	जारी रखना	Discontinue
32.	Difficult	कठिन	Easy
33.	Diligent	परिश्रमी	Idle
34.	Death	मृत्यु	Birth
35.	Despair	निराश	Hope
36.	Earn	कमाना	Spend
37.	Empty	खाली	Full
38.	Friendly	मित्रवत्	Hostile
39.	Freedom	स्वतंत्रता	Slavery
40.	Fame	यश	Defame
41.	Famous	प्रसिद्ध	Notorious
42.	Fickle	चंचल	Constant
43.	Final	अंतिम	Initial
44.	Finite	निश्चित	Infinite
45.	Fresh	ताजा	Stale
46.	False	झूठ	True
47.	Fertile	उपजाऊ	Barren
48.	Firm	दृढ़	Weak
49.	Foul	अशुद्ध	Fair

Sl. No.	*Word*	*Meaning*	*Antonyms*
50.	Fear	भय	Courage
51.	Glory	यश	Shame
52.	Genuine	असली	Duplicate
53.	Giant	विशालकाय	Dwarf
54.	Grant	स्वीकारना	Refuse
55.	Glad	प्रसन्न	Sad
56.	Grave	गंभीर	Cheerful
57.	General	सामान्य	Particular
58.	Guilty	अपराधी	Innocent
59.	Gentle	सभ्य	Rude
60.	Humble	विनम्र	Proud
61.	Happiness	प्रसन्नता	Misery
62.	Haste	जल्दी	Delay
63.	Hate	घृणा	Love
64.	Heavy	भारी	Light
65.	Heaven	स्वर्ग	Hell
66.	Handsome	सुंदर	Ugly
67.	Increase	बढ़ाना	Decrease
68.	Ignorance	अज्ञानता	Knowledge
69.	Import	आयात	Export
70.	Include	शामिल करना	Exclude
71.	Illiterate	अनपढ़	Educate
72.	Junior	कनिष्ठ	Senior
73.	Keen	उत्सुक	Dull
74.	Lament	उदार	Strict
75.	Lie	झूठ	Truth
76.	Loose	ढ़ीला	Tight
77.	Long	लम्बा	Short
78.	Loud	जोर से	Low

Sl. No.	Word	Meaning	Antonyms
79.	Lend	उधार	Borrow
80.	Laugh	हंसना	Weep
81.	Lead	नेतृत्व	Follow
82.	Limited	सीमित	Unlimited
83.	Minor	अल्पायु	Major
84.	Master	स्वामी	Servant
85.	Mad	पागल	Sane
86.	Material	भौतिक	Spiritual
87.	Majority	बहुमत	Minority
88.	Mistress	गृहणी	Maid
89.	Melody	लय	Discard
90.	Male	पुरुष	Female
91.	Masculine	पुलिंग	Feminine
92.	Neat	स्वच्छ	Dirty
93.	Native	देशवासी	Foreign
94.	Natural	प्राकृतिक	Artificial
95.	Nice	अच्छा	Nasty
96	Optimist	आशावादी	Pessimist
97.	Offensive	अतिकार	Deffensive
98.	Oral	मौखिक	Written
99.	Omission	लोभ	Commission
100.	Original	असल	Copy
101.	Ornamental	दिखावटी	Useful
102.	Offer	देना	Refuse
103.	Often	अक्सर	Seldom
104.	Prohibit	रोकना	Permit
105.	Precious	कीमती	Worthless
106.	Plenty	बहुत	Scarcity
107.	Profit	लाभ	Loss

Sl. No.	Word	Meaning	Antonyms
107.	Pride	घमण्ड़	Humility
109.	Punish	दण्ड देना	Reward
110.	Peace	शांति	War
111.	Permanent	स्थायी	Temporary
112.	Persuade	राजी करना	Dissuade
113.	Pleasure	प्रसन्नता	Pain
114.	Pros	अच्छाई	Cons
115.	Quick	जल्दी	Slow
116.	Reject	अस्वीकार	Grant
117.	Religious	धार्मिक	Irreligious
118.	Rich	धनी	Poor
119.	Reap	काटना	Sow
120.	Retreat	पीछे हटना	Advance
121.	Recover	प्राप्त करना	Lose
122.	Reduce	कम करना	Increase
123.	Relief	आराम	Trouble
124.	Rough	खुरदरा	Smooth
125.	Renoun	प्रसिद्धि	Disgrace
126.	Ruler	शासक	Subject
127.	Roar	दहाड़ना	Whisper
128.	Simple	साधारण	Complex
129.	Savage	असभ्य	Civilised
130.	Strong	मजबूत	Weak
131.	Smile	मुस्कुराना	Frown
132.	Strange	अपरिचित	Familiar
133.	Sweet	मीठा	Sour
134.	Superior	श्रवढ़	Inferior
135.	Sea	संमुद्र	Land
136.	Sensible	समझदार	Insensible

Sl. No.	*Word*	*Meaning*	*Antonyms*
137.	Sick	बीमार	Healthy
138.	Sympathy	सहानुभूति	Antipathy
139.	Stern	कठोर	Mild
140.	Success	सफलता	Failure
141.	Thick	मोटा	Thin
142.	Top	चोटी	Bottom
143.	Tame	पालतू	Wild
144.	Tragedy	दुखांत	Comedy
145.	Victory	विजय	Defeat
146.	Virtue	गुण	Vice
147.	Wisdom	बुद्धिमानी	Folly
148.	Wide	चौड़ा	Narrow
149.	Able	योग्य	Unable
150.	Bathed	स्नान	Unbathed
151.	Complete	पूर्ण	Incomplete
152.	Cover	ढ़कना	Uncover
153.	Direct	प्रत्यक्ष	Indirect
154.	Digest	पचाना	Indigest
155.	Equal	समान	Unequal
156.	Formal	नियमित	Informal
157.	Guide	मार्ग दर्शन	Misguide
158.	Human	मानवीय	Inhuman
159.	Just	न्याय संगत	Unjust
160.	Legal	कानूनी	Illegal
161.	Order	क्रम	Disorder
162.	Usual	साधारण	Unusual

86th days

(Vocabulary — शब्द कोश)

(अ)

1.	अंकुर	Nao, Sprout, Shoot
2.	अंकुश	Hook, Good, Restrain, Control
3.	अंगड़ाई	Stretching, Twisting
4.	अंगार	Enbers
5.	अंगीठी	Braizier, Furnace
6.	अंजर पंजर	Usuno
7.	अंजलि	Handful, Folded
8.	अंटसंट	Absurd
9.	अंडबंड	Irrelevant, Nonsense
10.	अंतर्गत	Inner, Including, Circle, Under
11.	अन्तर्धान	Vanish, Disappear
12.	अंतर्वासी	Indoor
13.	अंदाज	Estimate, Jecture
14.	अंधाधुंध	Blindly, Indiscriminately
15.	अंधेर	Injustices, Outrage
16.	अकड़	Conceit, Vanity
17.	अकाल	Famine, Dreadful, Horrible, Premature
18.	अक्खड़	Rough, Undisciplined
19.	अखाड़ा	Ring

20.	अगवानी	Welcome, Reception
21.	अगाध	Very deep, Profound, Learning
22.	अचूक	Unfailing, Infallible
23.	अचेत	Sleepy, Unconscious
24.	अटल	Affirm, Promise
25.	अडंगा	Obstacle, Impediment
26.	अडिग	Unflinching, Steady
27.	अडियल	Willful, mulish
28.	अत्याचार	Tyranny, Oppress
29.	अथक	Untiring
30.	अधीर	Impatient, restive
31.	अनंत	Endless, Unending
32.	अनबन	Rupture, Rift, Discord
33.	अनमना	Absent Minded
34.	अनहोनी	Improbable
35.	अनाचार	Malpractice, Misconduct
36.	अनाड़ी	Unskillful
37.	अनुचित	Improper
38.	अनुनय	Entreaty
39.	अनुराग	Attachment, Affection
40.	अनूठा	Uncommon, Singular
41.	अनेकता	Diversity
42.	अनौपचारिक	Informal
43.	अपकार	Harm, ill
44.	अपमानित	Infame
45.	अपजक	Unwinking
46.	अपवाद	Exception
47.	अपशगुन	Illomen
48.	अपार	Limitless, Boundless
49.	अपेक्षा	Compared

50.	अप्रिय	Unpleasant
51.	अबोध	Innocent
52.	अभय	Fearless
53.	अभिनंदन	Felicitation, Hearty, Commemoration
54.	अभिनव	New
55.	अभिवादन	Greeting
56.	अभूतपूर्ण	Unprecedented
57.	अर्थी	Bier
58.	अराजकता	Lawlessness, Anarchy
59.	अवगुण	Demerit
60.	अशुभ	Inauspicious, Indication
61.	अहोभाग्य	Good fortune, Good luck

(आ)

62.	आंख मिचौली	Hide and seek
63.	आंगन	Court Yard
64.	आंचल	Border, Clothe
65.	अभिवाय	Irrelevantly, Paintlessly
66.	आकांक्षा	Aspiration
67.	आगजनी	Arson
68.	आचार	Manners
69.	आजीवन	Lifelong, Throughout
70.	आजीविका	Livelihood
71.	आडंबर	Ostentation, Outward show
72.	आड़	Shelter, Cover
73.	आतंक	Terror
74.	आततायी / तानाशाह	Tyrant
75.	आत्मज्ञान	Self Realization
76.	आत्मत्याग	Self Sacrifice
77.	आत्मनिंदा	Self Condemnation

78.	आत्मनिर्णय	Self Determination
79.	आत्मनिर्भर	Self-reliant, Self-sufficient, Self-dependent
80.	आत्मप्रशंसा	Self praise
81.	आत्मरक्षा	Self defence
82.	आत्मविश्वास	Self Confidence
83.	आत्मसंतोष	Self Content
84.	आत्मसमर्पण	Surrender
85.	आत्मसम्मान	Self Respect
86.	आत्मीय	Intimate
87.	आत्मोद्धार	Self Salvation
88.	आन–बान	Pomp and Show
89.	आपदा	Misfortune, Calamity
90.	आपबीती	Self Experience
91.	आपसदारी	Mutual Relationship
92.	आपसी	Mutual, Private
93.	आपाधापी	Self Interest, Madrace
94.	आफत	Calamity, Distress
95.	आबरु	Honour, Dignity
96.	आबाद	Inhabitated, peopled
97.	आभार	Obligation, Gratefulness
98.	आभास	Hint, Inklink
99.	आमना सामना	Encounter
100.	आमने सामने	Face to Face
101.	आया गया	Visitor
102.	आयोजक	Convener
103.	आरंभिक	Initial, Preliminary
104.	आरती	Worship with lamps
105.	आर–पार	Across
106.	आरोप	Charge, Allegation

105.	आलोचक	Critic
106.	आवभगत	Hospitality, Entertainment
107.	आवा / भट्ठा	Kiln
108.	आवारा	Tramps, Vagabond, Loafer, Stray
109.	आवारा गर्दी	Loafing, Loitering, Vagraney
110.	आवाहन	Call invocation
111.	आशंका	Fear, Apprenhension
112.	आविर्भाव	Advent
113.	आशीर्वाद	Blessing
114.	आश्रम	Harmitage, Home
115.	आश्रय	Shelter, Harbour
116.	आसपास	Hearabout
117.	आसरा	Shelter, Support
118.	आस्था	Faith, Devotion
119.	आहिस्ता	Slowly, Gradually, Gently
120.	आव्हाद	Repture, Delight

(इ)

121.	इंतजाम	Management
122.	इंद्रिय	Organ of sense
123.	इंसाफ	Justice
124.	इच्छा	Will, Desire
125.	इच्छापात्र	Deed
126.	इच्छा शक्ति	Will Power
127.	इच्छित	Desired
128.	इच्छुक	Desirous willing
129.	इठलाना	Strut
130.	इर्द गिर्द	All About
131.	इकलौता	Only

(ई)

131.	ईमान	Faith, Integrity, Honesty, Conscientiously
132.	ईर्ष्या	Jealously

(उ)

133.	उड़ेलना	Pour out
134.	उत्रृण	Free Debtfree
135.	उकड़ूं	Squat
136.	उकताहट / आलस	Boredom
137.	उकताना	Tired
138.	उकसाना	Provoke, Incite
138.	उखड़ा पुखड़ा	Disjointed, Displaced, Dislodged
139.	उखाड पछाड़	Intrigue
140.	उचक्का	Swindler, Sharper
141.	उजड्ड	Boorish, Uncouth
142.	उठाई गीर	Pilferer
143.	उत्पात	Mischief, Nuisance
144.	उत्पीडन	Oppression
145.	उथल पुथल	Unheaval, Commotion
146.	उदार	Liberal, Generous
147.	उदास	Sad, Dejected
148.	उद्घाटन	Opening, Inauguration
149.	उद्धार	Conlift, Renovate
150.	उद्यम	Effort, Venture
151.	उधेड़बुन	Dilemma, Indecisiveness
152.	उनींद्रा	Sleepy
153.	उन्मूलन	Uprooting, Abolition
154.	उपदेश	Sermon
155.	उपलक्ष्य	View to Inview of

156.	उपवन	Parks
157.	उपवास	Fast
158.	उपहास	Redicule
159.	उपाधि	Degree
160.	उपाय	Remedy
161.	उपेक्षा	Disregard, Overlooking
162.	उफान	Ebullition
163.	उबटन	Unquent toilet paste
164.	उभड़ना	Rise up, emerge
165.	उमंग	Zest, Gusto
166.	उमस	Sultriness
167.	उमेठना	Wring
168.	उम्मीद	Hope
169.	उलझन	Complication, Embarrass, Intricacy
170.	उलझा	Entangled, Engaged
171.	उलट पलट, उलटफेर	Reshuffle Change
172.	उल्टा पुल्टा	Topsy-turry
173.	उल्टा सीधा	Absurd
174.	उलीचना	Drainout
175.	उल्लंघन	Violation
176.	उसांस	Exhale, sigh

(ऊ)

177.	ऊंघ	Drowsiness, Dozing, Naping
178.	ऊखल	Wooden morter
179.	ऊटपंटाग	Absurd
180.	ऊधम	Uproar, Tumult
181.	ऊधमी	Mischievous
182.	ऊब	Bore
183.	ऊबड़ खाबड़	Uneven, Rugged

184.	ऊल जलूल	Absurd
185.	ऊषा	Dawn, Day Break
186.	ऊषर	Barren, Desert

(ए)

187.	एंडा बैंडा	Unsystematic, Irregularly
188.	एकचित	Like-minded, Attentive
189.	एक जुट	United
190.	एकटक	Unblinkingly
191.	एकमत	Agreed, Unanimous, Predicatively
192.	एकतरफा	Undeclined, onesided, Unilateral
193.	एकरुप	Uniform, Same
194.	एकसाथ	See under
195.	एकाग्र	Concentrated
196.	एकांत	Solitude, Seclusion
197.	एकाध	Twice just once
198.	एतराज	Objection
199.	एलान	Announcement
200.	एवज	Exchange, Substitute
201.	एहसान	Obligation
202.	एहसास	Feeling

(ऐ)

203.	ऐच्छिक	Voluntary, Optional
204.	ऐन	Exact
205.	ऐब	Fault, Defect
206.	ऐय्याश	Debauchery, Luxury, Lewd
207.	ऐरा गैरा	Alien, Stranger,
208.	ऐश	Luxury
209.	ऐसा–वैसा	Trifling Insignificant

(ओ)

210.	औछा	Mean
211.	ओझल	Predicative, out of sight
212.	ओट	Covering, Shelter
213.	ओर छोर	Beginning, and end
214.	ओहदा	Post, Rank

(औ)

215.	औंधा	Upside down, Overturned
216.	औकात	Capacity
217.	औना पौना	Below par
218.	औपचारिक	Formal
219.	औसत	Average

(क)

220.	कंकड़	Gravel, Pebble
221.	कंगन	Bracelet
222.	कंगाल	Poor, Pauper
223.	कंटीला	Thorny
224.	कंपकपी	Shiver, Quiver
225.	कटु	Bitter, Unpleasant
226.	कट्टर	Staunch, Bigoted
227.	कठपुतली	Puppet
228.	कड़क	Thunder
229.	कतराना	Avoid ,evade
230.	कद्र	Value, worth
231.	कदाचित	Perhaps May be that
232.	कपट	Deceit, Fraud, Terrible
233.	कपूत	Unworthy Son

234.	कफन	Shroud
235.	कम अक्कल	Stupid, Foolish
236.	कमरतोड़	Ardous, Stringent
237.	कमाल	Wonder
238.	कमीना	Mean
239.	करतूत	Doing, Misdeed
240.	करम	Fate, Lucky, Destiny, Fortunate
241.	कराह	Groan, Moon
242.	करुणा	Pity, Mercy, Compassion
243.	कलंक	Blemish, Slur, Disgrace
244.	कलकल	Murmur
245.	कसूर	Fault, Guilt
246.	कसौटी	Touchstone
247.	कहासुनी	Wrangling
248.	कांव कांव	Crowing
249.	काई	Moss, Algae
250.	काट छांट	Cutting and clipping
251.	काठी	Fame, Physique
252.	कामचोर	Shirker
253.	कारगर	Effective
254.	कालिख	Soot Black
255.	किलकारी	Outery
256.	कीर्तन	Devotional Singing
257.	कुढ़न	Fretting, Repining
258.	कुम्हलाना	Fade, Faint
259.	कुलीन	Well Born
260.	कूदफांद	Gambols
261.	कृतघ्न	Ungrateful
262.	कृतार्थ	Satisfied
263.	कृपापूर्ण	Kind

264.	कृपालु	Kind, Benign
265.	कोपल	Sprout
266.	कोटि	Grade, Rank
267.	कोडा	Whip Lash
268.	कोरा	Unused
269.	कोल्हु	Crusher
270.	कौंध	Flash
271.	क्रमबद्ध	Orderly
272.	क्रमशः	Gradually
273.	क्रमानुसार	Serially
274.	क्षणिक	Transitory, Momentary
275.	क्षमता	Competence
276.	क्षमा	Pardon
277.	क्षीण	Feeble Impair
278.	क्षुब्ध	Distressed, Agetated
279.	क्षोम / दुख	Distress

(ख)

280.	खंजर	Sword, Sugger
281.	खंडन	Contradiction, Refutation
282.	खचाखच	Overcrowded
283.	खटखट	Knock, Rapping
284.	खडकना	Rattle, Jingle
285.	खपरैल	Tile roof
286.	खर्राटा	Snore
287.	खलबली	Commotion, Turmoil
288.	खातिरदारी	Hospitality
289.	खाना तलाशी	House Search
290.	खिन्न	Depressed, Sad
291.	खिल खिलाना	Coughloudly

292.	खिलना	Bloom, Bloosom
293.	खिलवाड़	Fun, Joke
294.	खिल्जी	Fun
295.	खिसियाना	Embarrassed
296.	खींचतान	Tussle, Tugging
297.	खुराफात	Smut, Mischief
298.	खुर्राट	Shrewd, Cleaveransly
299.	खुल्लमखुल्ला	Openly, Publicly
300.	खुशखबरी	Goodness
301.	खुशदिल	Cheerful
302.	खुसुर पुसुर	Whispering
303.	खूनी	Blood Thirsty
304.	खून पसीना	Blood and Sweat
305.	खेद	Regret
306.	खैर	Welfare
307.	खोट	Alloy Flaw, Deffect
308.	खौफ	Dread
309.	ख्याति	Fame, Reputation
310.	ख्वाह म ख्वाह	Unnecessarily
311.	ख्वाहिश	Wish, Desire, Acute

(ग)

312.	गंठजोड़	Alliance, Lineup
313.	गठबंधन	Secret, Alliance
314.	गंवार	Rustic
315.	गठीला	Robust
316.	गड़गड़ाना	Rumble, Thunder
317.	गड्ड मड्ड	Confusing, Muddle
318.	गद् गद्	Overwhelmed
319.	गपशप	Tittle, Tattle, Chit chat

320.	गपोड़ा	Gossip, Rumour
321.	गफलत	Negligence,
322.	गरमागरमी	Disputation
323.	गलतफहमी	Misunderstanding
324.	गाजा बाजा	Pomp and show
325.	गाना बजाना	Festivity
326.	गिचपिच	Crowding
327.	गिटपिट	Chattering
328.	गिड़गिड़ाना	Entreat, Implore
329.	गिरते पड़ते	Tottering, Manner
330.	गुंडा गर्दी	Hoolliganism
331.	गुच्छेदार	Bunchy, Tufty
332.	गुजर बसर	Live, Subsist
333.	गुटबंदी	Groupism, Factionism
334.	गुड़गुड़ाना	Bubbling
335.	गुनगुनाना	Humming, to hum
336.	गुलेल	Pellet Bow
337.	गुल्ली डंडा	Tip-cat
338.	गोपनीय	Confidential
339.	गोरख धंधा	Complication
340.	गोलमाल	Bungling
341.	गोल मटोल	Corpulent
342.	ग्रस्त	Affected, Stricken
343.	ग्रहण	Eclipse
344.	ग्रास	Morsel
345.	ग्लानि	Depression
346.	ग्वाला	Cowherd, Milk Man
347.	ग्वालिन	Milkmaid

(घ)

348.	घंटाघर	Clocktower
349.	घंटेवार	Hourly
350.	घटना बढ़ना	Fluctuate, Vary
351.	घनघोर	Thick, Dense
352.	घनचक्कर	Blockhead, Solt
353.	घनिष्ठता / घनिष्ठ	Intimate
354.	घमासान	Fierce
355.	घरबारी	Householder
356.	घराना	Dynasty, Family
357.	घसीट	Serawl, Seribble
358.	घाट	Ferry, Wharf
359.	घात	Ambuscade
360.	घात	Hurt
361.	घिघियाना	Falter
362.	घिचपिच	Clumsy
363.	घिन	Odium, Abhorrence
364.	घिसघिस	Dilly Dallging, Dilatoriness
365.	घिसापिटा	Wormout, Hackneyed
366.	घुडकना	Browbeat
367.	घुमंतु	Roving, Wandering
368.	घुमावदार	Winding, Circuitous
369.	घुसेड़ना	Thrust into, to pierce
370.	घूघंट	Veil, Face
371.	घूंट	Draught
372.	घूसेबाजी	Fisticuffs
373.	घूसा	Frown
374.	घूस	Bribe, illegal, Gratification
375.	घेरा	Siege
376.	घोंटना	Pound, Pulverize
377.	घोर	Awfulness

(च)

378.	चंगुल	Talon
379.	चंचल	Unsteady, Restless
380.	चंडाल	Low born
381.	चंदन	Sanders, Sandal Wood
382.	चंदा	Subscription
383.	चपत	Disappeared, Vanished
384.	चंवर	Whisk
385.	चकमा	Dodge
386.	चकल्लस	Drollery Comicality
387.	चकाचक	Fully, Completely
388.	चकाचौंध	Dazzle, Glare
389.	चखचख	Altercation, Noisy, Wrangler
390.	चटपट	Instantly, Immediately
391.	चतुर्मुखी	Foursided, Allround
392.	चपल	Restless
393.	चपलता	Restireness
394.	चपेट	Blow, Rap
395.	चमाचम	Brightly
396.	चरपरा	Pungent, Piquaint
397.	चाम	Extreme
398.	चराचर	Movable & Immovable, Animate & Inanimate
399.	चसका	Vice, Bad habit
400.	चहल पहल	Hustle and Bustle
401.	चापलूस	Sycaphant, Flatterer
402.	चालबाज	Crafty Trickster, Cunning
403.	चिंघाड	Trumpet
404.	चिकना चुपड़ा	Well groomed

405.	चिड़ चिड़ा	Peevish, Irritable
406.	चिता	Pyre, Funeral Pile
407.	चित्तवृति	Mood
408.	चिमटा	Shred, Remnant
409.	चिपचिपा	Visied, Sticky
410.	चिरस्थाई	Enduring, Lasting
411.	चिरस्मरणीय	Ever Memorable
412.	चुलबुला	Naughty
413.	चीख	Shriek, Scream
414.	चुगलखोर	Backbiter, sneak, Tell tale
415.	चुटकी	Pinch, Taunt, Snap
416.	चुड़ैल	Witch, Shrew
417.	चुपडमा	Daub, Smear
418.	चुलबुला	Frolicsoune, Sportine
419.	चुल्लू	Handful
420.	चुस्की	Sip
421.	चूड़ीदार	Puckered
422.	चूतिया	Foolish, Dolt, Dunce, Stupid
423.	चोंचला	Blandishment, Cyolery
424.	चोंचलेबाज	Coquettes, Prude
425.	चोला	Garb, Robe
426.	चोली	Bodice
427.	चौकना	Startled
428.	चौकस	Cautious
429.	चौखंटा	Quadrangular
430.	चौपाया	Quadruped
431.	चौफेर	On all sides
432.	चौरस	Level
433.	चौहदडी	Boundary
434.	चौहेरा	Fourfold

(छ)

435.	छन्द	Verse
436.	छक्का पंजा	Tactics
437.	छटपटाना	Writhe
438.	छटा	Beauty, Splendour
439.	छत्ता	Hive
440.	छत्र छाया	Protection, Patronage
441.	छद्म	Fraud, Preudonym, Disguise, Samouflage
442.	छपछपाना	Splash
443.	छबीला	Foppish, Comedy, Dandy, Handsome
444.	छरहरा	Thin and Tall, Smart
445.	छलावा	Illusion
446.	छलिया	Cheat
447.	छवि	Beauty, Winsouness
448.	छाप	Impression
449.	छिछला	Shallow
450.	छिछोरा	Friolous
451.	छिटपुट	Stray, Sporadic
452.	छिन्न भिन्न	Broken, Shattered, Scattered
453.	छिपे छिपे	Stealthily
454.	छौंका	Hanging
455.	छींट	Calico
456.	छींटा	Drop, Spot
457.	छीछालेदर	Humiliation
458.	छीना झपटी	Scramble
459.	छुआछूत	Untouchability
460.	छुटपन	Infancy, Childhood
461.	छुट्टा	Isolated, Single
462.	छूत	Contagion

463.	छेकना	Enclose
464.	छेड़खानी	Teasing, Disturbed, Picks and Franks
465.	छौंकना	Spice, Season

(ज)

466.	जंजाल	Entanglement
467.	जखीरा	Stock
468.	जखीरेबाज	Hoarder
469.	जगमग	Refulgent, Shining
470.	जगहँसाई	Popular, ridicule, Public Mockery
471.	जटा	Matted hair, Tangled hair
472.	जड़ाऊ	Inlaid
473.	जत्था	Band
474.	जनजागरण	Public consciousness
475.	जनवादी	Democratic
476.	जनमत	Public opinion, plebiscite
477.	जनशक्ति	Manpower
478.	जनसंपर्क	Public relation
479.	जनसंहार	Man slaughter
480.	जनहित	Public interest
481.	जप	Reading, Muttering
482.	जपतप	Prayers, worship and penances
483.	जय	Victory
484.	जलमग्न	Submerged
485.	जल यात्रा	Voyage
486.	जलसा	Meeting
487.	जल्दबाज	Hasty
488.	जल्लाद	Hangman
489.	जागीर	Fiet
490.	जानलेवा	Fatal, Deadly

491.	जाहिर	Obvious
492.	जिक्र	Mention
493.	जिज्ञासु	Inquisitive
494.	जिद्	Obstinacy
495.	जिद्दी	Obdurate
496.	जुगाली	Remunation, Chew
497.	जूझना	Struggle
498.	जूठन	Leaving, Defiled
499.	जोखिम	Hazardous
500.	जोगी	Ascetic
501.	जोड़ तोड़	Machination
502.	जोड़ीदार	Comrades
503.	जोर जुल्म	Oppression
504.	जोर शोर	Tempo Gush
505.	जोशीला	Ardent, Jealous
506.	ज्यादिती	Excesses, Highhandedness
507.	ज्योति	Light, Lusture
508.	ज्वलंत	Shining, Burning

(झ)

509.	झंकार	Trinkling, Tingling, Rattling
510.	झंझट	Trouble, Imbroglio, annoying
511.	झकझक	Wrangling
512.	झज्झर	Goblet
513.	झट	Instantly, Quickly
514.	झड़प	Skirmish, Snap, Cockfight
515.	झड़ी	Nonstop, Shower, Volley
516.	झपकना	Wink, Blink
517.	झमेला	Imbroglio
518.	झाड़पोछ	Brushing, Cleaning

519.	झाड़ू	Broom
520.	झापड़	Slap
521.	झालर	Frill, Ruffle, Frimbia
522.	झिझक	Hesitation, Shyness
523.	झुटपुटा	Dusk, Twilight
524.	झूमना	Sway
525.	झोंका	Gust, Whiff, Breeze, Stumble, Nap

(ट)

526.	टंटा	Wrangling
527.	टकटकी	Stare, Gaze
528.	टकराव	Clash
529.	टकसाल	Mint
530.	टकसाली	Genuine
531.	टक्कर	Collision
532.	टटोलना	Grope
533.	टपाटप	In succession
534.	टम टमाहट	Flickering, Twinkling
535.	टर्राना	Croak
536.	टांकना	Stich
537.	टांप टांय	Prattling,
538.	टालमटोल	Erasion, Putting off
539.	टीका	In occilation
540.	टीम टाम	Show
541.	टुकुर टुकुर	Stare-longly
542.	टुटपुजिंया	Meargemeans
543.	टूक	A pert reply
544.	टूटफूट	wear and tear
545.	टेक	Prop, Support
546.	टेकना	Bean, Shoulder

547.	टेढ़ा	Skrew, Curved
548.	टोंटी	Spout, Nozzle
549.	टोक	Hindrance, Interruption
550.	टोना टोटका	Black art, witchcraft, sorcery
551.	टोह	Search, look, trace, find out

(ठ)

552.	ठग	Cheat, Thug, Swindler
553.	ठठ्ठा	Joke, Jest
554.	ठस	Strongly, Built
555.	ठसाहस	Stuffed, Packed
556.	ठहाका	Loud Laugh
557.	ठाठ	Magnificence, Pomp
558.	ठाठबाट	Luxury, Pomp and show
559.	ठानना	Resolve
560.	ठूंठ	Stump, Amputate
561.	ठूसंना	Cran, Stuff fully
562.	ठेंगा	Contempt, Refusal
563.	ठेलना	Shone, Propel,
564.	ठेस	Hurt, Blow,
565.	ठोकना	Hammer

(ड)

566.	डंक	Bite, Sting
567.	डकार	Belching, Erectation
568.	डगमग	Roll, Staggering, Flattering
569.	डरावना	Dreadful
570.	डांट	Rebuke, Chide, Scold, Reprimand
571.	डींग	Boast, Brag, Vaunt
572.	डीढ	Mesmerize

573.	डुगडुगी	Tom Tom Tabor
574.	डुबकी	Dip, Dive, Plunge
575.	डोला	Litter

(ढ)

576.	ढकोसला	Humbug
577.	ढाडस	Fortitude
578.	ढाल	Shield
579.	ढिठाई	Audacity, Imputance, Pertness
580.	ढिलाई	Laxity, Slackness
582.	ढुलमुल	Shady, Slack
583.	ढोंग	Trick, Fraud
584.	ढोंगी	Hypocritical, Fraudulent

(त)

585.	तंग	Tight
586.	तंगी	Shortage, Want
587.	तटस्थ	Heutral
588.	तड़कभड़क	Glitters
589.	तड़ातड़	Rapid Succession
590.	तना	Bole, Trunk, Stem
591.	तनातनी	Tension
592.	तन्मय	Engrossed, Preoccupied, Absorbed
593.	तप	Penance, Asceticism
594.	तपस्वी	Ascetic, Harmit
595.	तबला	Tambourine
596.	तमतमाना	To get rid of, To redden
597.	तमाचा	Slap
598.	तमीज	Decorum, Etiquette
599.	तरबतर	Soaked, Drenched

600.	तहस–नहस	Ruined, Devastated
601.	ताक–झांक	Peeping
602.	तामझांम	Paraphernalia
603.	तिकडम	Unfairmeans, Manoeuvred Device
604.	तू तडाक	Wrangle
605.	तृष्णा	Craving
606.	तेज दिमाग	Quick Temper
607.	तेजस्वी	Imposing
608.	तोड़ फोड़	Sabotage
609.	तोड़म फोड़	Distortion
610.	त्रुटि	Short coming, Defect

(थ)

611.	थका मंदा	Jaded, Worn and Wearied
612.	थकान	Tired, Fatigue, Exhaust, Weary
613.	थपकना	Pat
614.	थप्पड़	Slap, Spank,
615.	थर थर	Trembling, Shivering, Shuddering
616.	थाती	Trust, Charge
617.	थामना	To hold,
618.	थाल	Platter
619.	थाह	Depth
620.	थुथना	Nozzle, Snout
621.	थूक	Sputum, Spittle
622.	थोंपना	Impose, thrust

(द)

623.	दंगल	Wrestling, Bout, Tournament
624.	दंगा	Riot
625.	दंभ	Vanity, conceit

626.	दखल	Possession
627.	दंगा	Treachery, Perfidy, Deceit
628.	दड़वा	Coop
629.	दंत्तचित्त	Fully Attentive
630.	दबंग	Bold, Dauntless
631.	दबोचना	Pounce upon, Swoop down, upon
632.	दम दिलासा	False hope, Vain, consolation
633.	दमन	Suppression
634.	दमनकरी	Repressive
635.	दयनीय	Pitiable
636.	दया दृष्टि	Kind, attitude, Kindness, Attention
637.	दरार	Crack, Fissure
638.	दरिद्र	Poor, Pauper
638.	दलदल	Quagmire, Bog, Swamp, Marsh
640.	दानापानी	Food and drink, Subsistence
641.	दानेदार	Granular
642.	दिवंगत	Deceased
643.	दीवाना	Crazy
644.	दुखड़ा	Woes, Tale of Suffering
645.	दुत्कारना	Rebuke, Reproach, Indignantly, snub
646.	दुभाषिया	Bilinguist, Interpretor
647.	दुरावस्था	Sad plight, Miserable Condition, Predicament
648.	दुराग्रह	Obstinacy
649.	दुराव	Concealment
650.	दुर्गन्ध	Stench, Foul, Bad smell
651.	दुर्गम	Inaccessible
652.	दुर्गुण	Vice, Defect
653.	दुर्भावना	Ill will, Malice

654.	दुर्भिक्ष	Famine, Drought
655.	दुर्लभ	Rare, Scarce, Unavailable
656.	दुर्व्यसन	Vice, Evil habit, addict
657.	दुलार	Cosseting, Fondling
658.	दुविधा	Dilemma, Fix, Suspence, Uncertainty
659.	दुस्साहस	Imputance
660.	दूधपूत	Men and Money
661.	दूरगामी	Far reaching
662.	दूरदर्शिता	Forsightness
663.	दूषित	Contaminated, Defiled
664.	दृष्टांत	Instance
665.	देशद्रोह	Treason
666.	देश निकाला	Deportation, Exile, Banish
667.	दोगला	Crossbred, Mongrel
668.	द्वंद	Duel fight
669.	द्विपक्षीय	Bilateral

(ध)

670.	धक्का पेल	Jostle
671.	धक्का मुक्की	Pushing and elbowing
672.	धज्जी	Shred, strip
673.	धडाधड़	Quick
674.	धड़ाम	Thud
675.	धत्	Fie
676.	धनधान्य	Affluence, Alround Pros perity
677.	धन्नासेठ	Moneyed person
678.	धन्य	Blessed
679.	धमकाना	Intimidale Threaten
680.	धमाचौकड़ी	Gambol, Turmoil, hustles-bustle
681.	धमाधम	Constant thumping bound

681.	धांधली	High handedness
682.	धाक	Overwhelming
683.	धाकड़	Dashing, Dauntless
684.	धाराप्रवाह	Fluently, Nonstop
685.	धावा	Sortie, Sudden attack
686.	धिक्कार	Condemnation, Censure
687.	धींगा मस्ती	Scuffle
688.	धुंध	Hage, Mist, Fog
689.	धुन	Craze
690.	धुरंधर	Preeminent
691.	धूम	Boom, Pomp
692.	धूर्त	Crooked, Knave cunning
693.	ध्रष्टता	Insolence, Arrogance, Impudent
694.	धौंस	Threat, Cheat, Bluster
695.	धौंसपट्टी	Threating
696.	ध्वस्त	Devastated, Wrecked

(न)

697.	नंग धंड़गा	Star naked
698.	नकटा	Noseless
699.	नटखट	Coquetry
700.	नगण्य	Negligible, Insignificant
701.	नजरबंद	Interned
702.	नत्थी	Linking
703.	नमकहराम	Unfaithful, Ungrateful, disloyal
704.	नमकहलाल	Faithful, Loyal, Grateful
705.	नरम गरम	Up and down, good and fade
706.	नवनिर्माण	Reconstruction
707.	नवरस	Nine Sentiments
708.	नांद	Trough

709.	नाकारा	Useless, Worthless
710.	नाजायज	Improper
711.	नाम निशान	Trace, Vestige
712.	नाशवान	Perishable
713.	निदंनीय	Condemnable, Reprehensible
714.	निकृष्ट	Base, Low
715.	निखटटू	Indolent, Drone, Idle
716.	निरंकुश	Autocratic, Despotic
717.	निराकार	Formless
718.	निर्जन	Uninhabited, Desert
719.	निष्फल	Abortive, Ineffective
720.	निःसंतान	Issueless, without Progency
721.	नीयत	Intention
722.	नीम हकीम	Quack
723.	नेक चलन	Good Conduct
724.	नोक झोंक	Altercation
725.	नौसिखिया	Novice
726.	न्याय	Distract

(प)

727.	पंखुडी	Petal
728.	पंगु	Crippled
729.	पंडाल	Pavilion
730.	पक्षपात	Partiality, Prejudice
731.	पगडंडी	Track, Footpath
732.	पचडा	Muddle
733.	पच्चर	Wedge
734.	पटरानी	Queen, Consort
735.	पतिव्रता	Faithful wife
736.	परचून	Retail

737.	परत	Layer
738.	परस्पर	Mutual, Reciprocal
739.	परहेज	Abstinence
740.	पराकाष्ठा	Extreme, Culminating point
741.	पराक्रम	Valour, Gallant
742.	परिमार्जित	Refined
743.	परी	Fairy
744.	परोपकार	Benevolence
745.	पश्चाताप	Repentance, Penitence
746.	पहेली	Riddle
747.	पाखण्ड	Hypocrisy, Dissimulation
748.	पाजी	Rascal, Wicked
749.	पात्र	Utensil
750.	पारखी	Connoiseur Judge
751.	पास पास	Close
752.	पिछवाड़ा	Rear Back
753.	पिल पिला	Flaccid, Flabby
754.	पुचकारना	Caress, Fondle
755.	पुण्य	Righteous, Action, Virtue
756.	पुनर्उद्धार	Regeneration, Reclamation
757.	पुरुषार्थ	Manliness, Courage
758.	पुलकित	Horripilated
759.	पुष्पांजलि	Floral tribute
760.	पुष्पित	Floriferous, Flowery
761.	पूज्य	Reverable
762.	पैतृक	Ancestral
763.	प्रकोप	Fury
764.	प्रचण्ड	Fierce, Violent
765.	प्रण	Vow, Pledge

766.	प्रतिबद्ध	Committed
767.	प्रतिशोध	Revenge, Avenge
768.	प्रभुत्व	Mastery
769.	प्रहार	Assault
770.	प्राणघातक	Deadly
771.	प्रायश्चित	Atonement
772.	प्रारब्ध	Fate, Luck
773.	प्रोत्साहन	Encouragement, Incentive

(फ)

774.	फंदा	Trap
775.	फटकार	Rebuke, Reprimand
776.	फण	Hood
777.	फतवा	Decree, Verdict
778.	फुरफुर	Swiftly, Quickly
779.	फरमाइश	Request
780.	फरार	Absconding
781.	फरियाद	Supplication
782.	फर्जी	Fictitious
783.	फर्राटा	Hurry
784.	फसाद	Brawl, Quarrel
785.	फांकना	Chuck in
786.	फिरकी	Spool
787.	फिलहाल	For the present
788.	फुंकार	Hissing
789.	फुदकना	Hop
790.	फुरती	Agility, Smartness
791.	फुर्र	Flutter
792.	फुॅसफुसा	Flabby
793.	फुसलाना	Allure, Entice

794.	फुहार	Drizzle
795.	फूंक	Puff
796.	फूट	Rift, Split
797.	फूहड़	Slovenly, Shabby
798.	फेंटना	Beat
799.	फेरफार	Suffling
800.	फेरबदल	Alteration

(ब)

801.	बंजर	Waste, Fallow
802.	बकझक	Jabber, Gabble
803.	बगावत	Revolt, Rouse, Stir up, put down, Suppress
804.	बटोरन	Sweaping
805.	बड़बड़	Grumble, Mutter
806.	बडबोला	Talkative, Garrulous
807.	बद्चलन	Depraved
808.	बद्तमीज	Illmanners
809.	बदमाश	Wicked
810.	बनाठना	Well groomed
811.	बर्दाश्त	Tolerance, Forbearance
812.	बरामद	Recovered
813.	बवंडर	Whirlwind, Cyclone
814.	बहार	Spring
815.	बहुरुपिया	Mimic, protean
816.	बागडोर	Control
817.	बाजारु	Common place, Market Square
818.	बाजी	Indulgence
819.	बाड	Fence, Hedge
820.	बाना	Costume, Dress
821.	बिलखना	Wail

822.	बिल दिलाना	Whine
823.	बिलोना	Churn
824.	बुदबुदा	Bubbles
825.	बूदाबांदी	Light Shower
826.	बूटी	Herb
827.	बेड़ी	Shackles, Irons
828.	बेढंगा	Clumsy, Slovenly
829.	बेतुका	Irrelevant, Absurd
830.	बेहद	Boundless
831.	बोझिल	Burdensome
832.	बोटी	Chop
833.	बौखलाना	Fret, Lose Temper

(भ)

834.	भंडा	Utensil
835.	भंटुआ	Procurer
836.	भंवर	Whirlpool
837.	भगदड़	Halter Skelter, Sla
838.	भगोड़ा	Fugitive, Absconder
839.	भट्टा	Kiln
840.	भड भेड़िया	Garrulous
841.	भडास	Spite ,Stored up
842.	भद्दा	Clumsy
843.	भन्वाना	Hum, Buzz
844.	भभकी	Hollow threat
845.	भरपूर	Abundant
846.	भरसक	Utmost
847.	भरापूरा	Complete, Flourshing
848.	भला चंगा	Hale and Hearty
849.	भलामानस	Noble, Gentleman

850.	भारी भरकम	Bulky
851.	भीड़भाड़	Hustle and Bustle
852.	भीषण	Horrible
853.	भुक्खड़	Varacious, Raverous
854.	भुखमरी	Starvation
855.	भुरता	Mesh
856.	भुरभुरा	Crisp
857.	भुलक्कड़	Forgetful
858.	भूलभूलैया	Maze
859.	भूला बिसरा	Ignored, Forgotten
860.	भूला भटका	Strayed, Losing the way
861.	भेदभाव	Discrimination
862.	भेष	Guise
863.	भोंदू	Silly
864.	भौंरा	Black bee
865.	भौंचक	Nonplussed, Dumbfounded
866.	भ्रम	Misconception, Confusion

(म)

867.	मंगल	Well being, Welfare
868.	मंगलमय	Blessed, Happy
869.	मंडराना	Hover
870.	मंत्र	Hymns, Incantation
871.	मक्कार	Cunning, Sly
872.	मक्खीचूस	Miser, niggardly
873.	मटर गस्त	Loitering
874.	मढना	Mout
875.	मतभेद	Dissension
876.	मतवाला	Intoxicated, Wayward
877.	मनगढ़त	Fabricated, Concoeted

878.	मनमाना	Arbritrary
879.	मनमानी	Willfulness
880.	मनमुटाव	Estrangement, Dissension
881.	मनमौजी	Self willed
882.	मनहूस	Unlucky, Ominous
883.	मनोरथ	Longing
884.	मनोहर	Captivating, Charming
885.	ममता	Affection
886.	मर्यादा	Decorum, Propriety
887.	मलाई	Scum
888.	मलाल	Compunction, Regret
889.	महक	Fragrance
890.	महिमा	Glory, Greatness
891.	मानभंग	Defamation
892.	मामूली	Ordinary
893.	माया	Illusion
894.	मारामारी	Rush, Bustle
895.	मिमियाना	Bleat
896.	मिलनसार	Effable, Sociable
897.	मिलना जुलना	Mix, Associate
898.	मुंहजोर	Headstrong
899.	मुहतोड़	Apt, Irrefutable
900.	मुंहफट	Out Spoken
901.	मुकुट	Coronet, Diadam
902.	मुदगर	Mallet, Club
903.	मूसलाधार	Torrents
904.	मूर्धन्य	Cerebral
905.	मृदु	Mild, Soft
906.	मेहमानदारी	Hospitality

907.	मेहरबान	Kind
908.	मोक्ष	Salvation
909.	मोच	Sprain
910.	मोरी	Drain, Sewar
911.	मोरचा	Rust
912.	मोलतोल	Haggling, Bargaining
913.	मोहन	Charming
914.	मोहित	Charmed
915.	मौन	Quiet, Silent

(य)

916.	यकीन	Faith, Confidence
917.	यकीनी	Sure, certain
918.	यथेष्ट	Ackquate
919.	यथोचित	Appropriate
920.	यश	Reputation, Fame
921.	याचना	Entreaty, Solicilation
922.	यातना	Torture, Torment
923.	युक्ति	Device
924.	युवराज	Crownprince
925.	योगी	Ascetic
926.	यौवन	Youth, Youthfulness

(र)

927.	रंगढंग	Way, Style, Manners
928.	रंगभूमि	Theatre
929.	रंगभेद	Colour, Prejudice, Aparthied
930.	रंगमंच	Stage
931.	रंगरेली	Revelry
932.	रंज	Grief

933.	रंडी	Prostitute
934.	रजामंदी	Consent
935.	रथ	Chariot
936.	रफूचक्कर	To slink away
937.	रमणीक	Pleasant
938.	रमना	To enjoy
939.	रवैया	Attitude
940.	रसा	Broth, Soup
941.	रसिक	Amorous
942.	रहन–सहन	Way of living
943.	रहासहा	Remaining
944.	राग	Melody, Amodo in music
945.	राग	Attachment
946.	रागरंग	Merrymaking
947.	राजतिलक	Coronation
948.	राजद्रोह	Sedition
949.	राजपाट	Reign
950.	राजवंश	Dynasty
951.	राजी	Willing
952.	राजी खुशी	Well and happy
953.	राज्यकाल	Regine, Period of rule
954.	राब	Treack, Mocasses
955.	रिझाना	Fascinate, Enchant
956.	रिमझिम	Drizzling
957.	रिसना	Trickle, Run
958.	रुझान	Inclination, Tendency
959.	रुनझुन	Twinkling
960.	रुठना	Offend, Sulk
961.	रेतना	File
962.	रेलपेल	Crowding

963.	रोमांच	Horripilation, Thrill
964.	रोष	Indignant, Resentment
965.	रौंदना	Trample
966.	रौनक	Brilliance

(ल)

967.	लंगोटिया	Close
968.	लगन	Devotion, Whole Heartedness, Auspicious
969.	लगभग	Approximately
970.	लचक	Elasticity, Flexible
971.	लचर	Foolish
972.	लजाना	Shy, Blush, Bashful
973.	लट	Tress, Wek
974.	लड़खड़ाना	Stagger, Faller, Stumble
975.	लताड़	Rebuke, Scolding, Chide
976.	लथपथ	Drenched
977.	लहंगा	Roguish
978.	लबड़धोधों	Chaotic, Confusion
979.	लय	Rhythm
980.	ललक	Longing, Yearning
981.	लल्लोचप्पो	Flattery
982.	लवलीन	Absorbed
983.	लस	Stickiness, Sliminess
984.	लहलहाना	Bloom, Flourish
985.	लांछन	Aspersion
986.	लांछित	Stigmatized
987.	लाचार	Helpless
988.	लाजवाब	Pearless, Matchless
989.	लाड़	Affection, Darling, Fonding

990.	लानत	Condemnation
991.	लालच	Greedy
992.	लालसा	Ardent desire, yearning
993.	लालायित	Wishful, Anxious
994.	लावारिस	Heirless
995.	लिदवाना	Plastered
996.	लीचड़	Stingy, miserly
997.	लुंज	Crippled
998.	लुच्चा	Vagrant
999.	लुभाना	Allure, Tempt, Entire
1000.	लूटखसोट	Spoil, Pillage, Plunder
1001.	लूला	Crippled, Maimed
1002.	लूलू	Nitwit, Idiot
1003.	लेन देन	Dealing
1004.	लौकिक	Wordly

(व)

1005.	वक्तृत्व	Oratory
1006.	वचनबद्ध	Committed
1007.	वज्र	Thunderbolt
1008.	वनवास	Exile
1009.	वर्जित	Disallowed
1010.	वर्ण विचार	Phonemics
1011.	वश	Control, Hold
1012.	वहम	Misconception
1013.	वहमी	Superstition
1014.	वहशी	Savage
1015.	वांछित	Desired
1016.	वादविवाद	Debate
1017.	वान	Possessor

1018.	वापिसी	Refund
1019.	वारा न्यारा	Settlement, Change of Fortune
1020.	वासना	Passion
1021.	वाह वाह	Hurrah, Excellent
1022.	वाही तवाही	Nonsense
1023.	विकट	Formidable, Dreadful
1024.	विकल्प	Option
1025.	विकार	Disorder
1026.	विकृत	Unsound, Deformed
1027.	विक्षिप्त	Mad, Insane
1028.	विघटन	Disintegration, Dissolved
1029.	विघ्न	Interruption
1030.	विचलित	Upset, Deflect
1031.	विच्छेद	Curtailment
1032.	विश	Well Versed
1033.	विडंबना	Irony, Mockery
1034.	विद्रोह	Revolt, Rebellion
1035.	विद्वेष	Malice, Rancour
1036.	विधिवत	Methodically
1037.	विनत	Bowed down
1038.	विनम्र	Entreaty
1039.	विनम्रता	Humble, Courtious
1040.	विनय	Entreaty, Solicitation
1041.	विनोदी	Witty
1042.	विपरीत	On the contrary
1043.	विफल	Fruitless, Futile
1044.	विभूति	Outstanding
1045.	विभूषित	Adorned
1046.	विमल	Clear
1047.	विमुख	Disinclined

1048.	विखत	Detached
1049.	विरला	Rare
1050.	विलक्षण	Queer, Peculiar, Fantastic
1051.	विवेक	Discretion
1052.	विवेकपूर्ण	Judicious
1053.	विषम	Odd
1054.	विहार	Enjoyment, Pleasure
1055.	वीर्य	Semen
1056.	वेदी	Altar
1057.	वेश	Garb, Guise
1058.	वेशभूषा	Makeup
1059.	वैर	Enmity, Hostility
1060.	व्यंग	Snear, Gibe
1061.	व्यथा	Agony, Distress
1062.	व्यभिचार	Debouchery, Adultery
1063.	व्यसन	Evil habit, Vice
1064.	व्यसनी	Dissolute
1065.	व्याकुल	Perturbed, upset

(श)

1066.	शंका	Misgiving, suspicion, doubt
1067.	शहर	Decency, Manners
1068.	शगुन	Omen, Augury
1069.	शरण	Refuge, Shelter
1070.	शर्मिंदा	Ashamed, Remorseful
1071.	शान	Magnificance, Grandeur, Splendour
1072.	शाप	Curse, Imprecation
1073.	शाबास	Excellent, Bravo, Well done, Applause
1074.	शामत	Adversity, Misfortune
1075.	शामियाना	Canopy

1076.	शाही	Royal
1077.	शिकंजा	Clamp
1078.	शिखर	Peak, Summit
1079.	शिथिल	Slack, Lax
1080.	शिष्ट	Decent, Polite, Decorum
1081.	शील	Moral, Conduct
1082.	शुभ	Auspicious
1083.	शुभचिंतक	Well wisher
1084.	शोक	Grief, Sorrow
1085.	शोचनीय	Deplorable
1086.	शोभा	Grace, Elegance
1087.	शौक	Fondness
1088.	शौकिया	Amateur
1089.	शौकीन	Dandy, Fop
1090.	श्रद्धांजलि	Homage
1091.	श्रद्धा	Veneration
1092.	श्रद्धेय	Revered
1093.	श्रेष्ठ	Excellent, Best

(ष)

1094.	षडयंत्र	Plot, Conspiracy

(स)

1095.	संकल्प	Resolution, Resolve, Determination
1096.	संपत	Restrained
1097.	संयोग	Coincidence
1098.	संशोधन	Amendment
1099.	संस्कार	Rite, Ceremony
1100.	सस्मरण	Reminiscences, Memory
1101.	सकपकाना	Startled, Confounded

1102.	सकुशल	Safe
1103.	सगा	Real
1104.	सगाई	Engagement, Betrothal
1105.	सजधज	Pomposity
1106.	सजीला	Foppish
1107.	सज्जित	Furnished
1108.	सड़न	Putrefaction, Rotten
1109.	षडयंत्र	Stench, Putrid
1110.	सडियन	Perish
1111.	सनक	Craze, Frenzy
1112.	सनसनी	Sensation
1113.	सन्न	Stunned, Stupefied
1114.	सन्नाटा	Stillness
1115.	सबक	Lesson
1116.	समकालीन	Contemporary
1117.	संवेदना	Sympathy
1118.	समाधि	Trance, Meditation
1119.	समाना	Contain
1120.	समीक्षा	Review
1121.	समूचा	Whole, Entire
1122.	समुचित	Due, Proper
1123.	सरपट	Galloping, Apace
1124.	सरसरी	Cursory
1125.	सरासर	Perfect Sheer
1126.	सराहना	Praise, Applaud
1127.	सलूक	Treatment
1128.	सहलाना	Tickle
1129.	सहारे	Against
1130.	सहृदय	Tenderhearted
1131.	सहेजना	Entrust
1132.	सहोदर	Real brother

1133.	सांड	Stallion
1134.	सांत्वना	Solace, consolation
1135.	साख	Goodwill, Credit
1136.	साग	Potherb
1137.	साजिश	Plot, Intrigue
1138.	सादगी	Simplicity
1139.	सामाजिक	Timely
1140.	सामर्थ्य	Power
1141.	सार	Gist, Substance
1142.	सार्थक	Meaningful, Significant
1143.	साहसिक	Adventurous
1144.	सिसकना	Sob, Choke
1145.	सिहरन	Thrill
1146.	सीनाजोरी	Aggressiveness
1147.	सुखद	Pleasant
1148.	सुगम	Easy, Facilitated
1149.	सुघड़	Shapely, Wellbuilt, Wellformed
1150.	सुचारु	Fine
1151.	सुदूर	Remote, Very far off
1152.	सुधबुध	Senses, Conscious
1153.	सुनसान	Solitary, Desolate
1154.	सुपर्द	Entrust
1155.	सुयश	Renown, Reputation
1156.	सुरबुराना	Crawl, Creep
1157.	सुराग	Trace, Clue
1158.	सुरीला	Melodious
1159.	सुलगना	Smoulder
1160.	सुलगना	Kindle
1161.	सुलह	Reconciliation
1162.	सूझ	Vision, Imagination
1162.	सूनापन	Loneliness

1163.	सूली	Gibbel Gallows
1164.	सेंध	Hole
1165.	सेंधमार	Burglar
1166.	सेहना	Hatch
1167.	सेहरा	Diadem
1168.	सोंटा	Cudgel
1169.	सोंधा	Aromatic
1170.	सौंह	Oath, Swear
1171.	सौजन्य	Courtesy
1172.	सौत	Cowife
1173.	सौतेला	Halfblood
1174.	सौदा	Bargain
1175.	स्तब्ध	Stunned
1176.	स्तुति	Praise
1177.	स्पंदन	Vibration
1178.	स्पर्धा	Rivalry
1179.	स्फूर्ति	Agility, Smartness
1180.	स्वच्छंद	Free
1181.	स्वयं	Personally
1182.	स्वरुप	Natural
1183.	स्वल्प	Very Little
1184.	स्वाम	Impersonation
1185.	स्वावलंबी	Self Relying
1186.	स्वेच्छा	Voluntarily
1187.	स्वेच्छिक	Voluntary

(ह)

1188.	हंकार	Call, Shout
1189.	हंगामा	Tumult, Disturbance
1190.	हँसमुख	Joly
1191.	हंसीखुशी	Merriment

1192.	हंसोड़	Jocular
1193.	हकदार	Entitled
1194.	हकला	Stammerer
1195.	हक्का बक्का	Stupefied, Confounded
1196.	हट्टा कट्टा	Robust, Shout and strong
1197.	हठ	Stubborness, Obstinacy
1198.	हडपना	Misappropriate
1199.	हड़बड़ाना	Nonplussed, Confused
1200.	हड़बड़ी	Flurry, Confusion
1201.	हथकंड	Tricks, Tactics
1202.	हथकड़ी	Handcuffs
1203.	हमजोली	Companion
1204.	हरियाली	Greenery
1205.	हलचल	Stir, Commotion
1206.	हलवा	Pudding,
1207.	हलाल	Legitimate act
1208.	हवस	Uproar, Vigorously
1209.	हवन	Fire, Sacrifice
1210.	हवाखोरी	Enjoying
1211.	हवाला	Custody
1212.	हवालात	Lock up
1213.	हवेली	Mansion
1214.	हांफना	Pant
1215.	हाथापाई	Scuffle
1216.	हामी	Assent
1217.	हार्दिक	Heartly, Cordial
1218.	हाल चाल	General condition
1219.	हावी	Dominant
1220.	हाशिया	Margin
1221.	हासिल	Obtained
1222.	हास्य	Humour

1223.	हाहाकार	Loud, Commentation
1224.	हिंडोला	Cradled, Swing
1225.	हिचकोला	Jolt
1226.	हिजड़ा	Eunuch, Impotent person
1227.	हित	Interest
1228.	हितका	Beneficial
1229.	हितैषी	Well Wisher
1230.	हिनहिनाना	Neigh
1231.	हिलोरा	Surge
1232.	हुक्का	Hubble, Bubble
1233.	हुज्जत	Objection
1234.	हुड़दंग	Uproar
1235.	हुनर	Art, Skill
1236.	हुक	Shooting, Pain
1237.	हूबहू	Exact
1238.	हेकडी	Arrogance
1239.	हेठी	Humiliation
1240.	हेतु	Motive
1241.	हैवान	Beast
1242.	होनहार	Promising
1243.	होनी	Fate
1244.	होश	Consciousness
1245.	हौज	Reservoir
1246.	हौदी	Cistern
1247.	हौवा	Bogey, Bugbear
1248.	हौसला	Morale

"Infant longing east widest,
Content pacing west way,
Such on base of midest,
Else dead wish shore God! pray"

Jagram Singh